HOW TO BOIL AN EGG
184 simple recipes
for one

The Essential Book
for the First-Time Cook

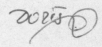

**WHAT READERS SAY ABOUT
HOW TO BOIL AN EGG**

'*The best cookbook ever*! I bought this when I first left home 20 years ago. It was exactly what I needed then as I could only cook using the microwave and toaster! Now it still gets regular use by both myself and my husband, particularly the Sunday Roast section. Highly recommended to anyone who needs the confidence to have a go.'

'Started at uni, barely a kitchen and this book taught me how to make those simple things when I really didn't have a clue. Next to copying someone else, it's the best way to learn and still helps me today.'

'*The first recipe book anyone should buy*. I was given this book when I went to university many many years ago. It's pretty much the only recipe book I have used consistently ever since. This book is a little gem and worth every single penny.'

'This book is great for first-time cooks but also for the more seasoned cook to be reminded of a long-lost cooking method. Now buying this for my sister who had to ring me to find out how to make scrambled egg for her and her baby boy!'

'I was given this book as a housewarming present when I first moved out of my parents' house about 15 years ago. This is a brilliant book for someone who needs to cook simple, tasty meals for one or two. The book is full of useful tips and the recipes are easy to follow. The spaghetti bolognese is one recipe that I remember with much fondness.'

'This book was my saviour. A first-class basic cookery book… Highly recommended!'

Originally for Jon, Jon,
whose architectural aspirations
inspired this book.

But now for the next generation
Amy, Jillian, Joanne and Alicia,
who will be off to Uni soon
and for Maya, Ben, Mia and Elaine
who'll be there later.

Welcome to Laura Rose,
who is catching up as fast as she can
– never forgetting Baby Sam.

Also, thank you to all my researchers
Amy, Jillian, Joanne, Elaine and Ed,
Annabel, Barbara, Jon and Iain,
for their helpful, amusing and interesting comments!

HOW TO
BOIL AN EGG
184 simple recipes
for one

Jan Arkless

RIGHT WAY

Constable & Robinson Ltd
3 The Lanchesters
162 Fulham Palace Road
London W6 9ER
www.constablerobinson.com

First published in the UK 1986

This new, completely revised and updated edition published by Right Way,
an imprint of Constable & Robinson, 2009

A copy of the British Library Cataloguing in Publication Data
is available from the British Library

ISBN: 978-0-7160-2220-6
Printed and bound in the EU

3 5 7 9 10 8 6 4 2

CONTENTS

INTRODUCTION

I originally wrote this book to help my son with his cooking when he first went to university. I have since realized that the recipes contained here are not only useful for students but for anyone, male or female, of any age, who finds themselves alone, and for the first time has to cook for themselves, whether in their own home or in new accommodation.

Now, over twenty years later, the book has been completely updated and revised with help from the next generation of students in the family, who have contributed even more handy hints and their favourite recipes.

It's amazing how our eating habits and the foods widely available have changed since the book was first written. Vegetables that used to be seasonal are now flown in from all over the world, and are available all year round – delicious strawberries, raspberries, peaches, mangoes, grapes, avocados and asparagus, tiny French beans and sugar snap peas to name but a few that were once strictly summertime treats. There are new variations of the old favourites – tiny new carrots, miniature cauliflowers and baby corn cobs, and so many varieties of lettuce and salad leaves. (Do you remember those flabby, round lettuces that were so difficult to wash?)

We now have beautiful fish from all round the globe, including many varieties that were once only available to eat in smart restaurants. Meat is sold ready prepared for cooking, either fresh from the butcher or in chilled or frozen packets, and cartons of ready meals fill the supermarket shelves. Dairy products – cheeses of all kinds, yogurts, cream and crème fraîche – and delicious desserts are all there on the shelves ready to be used to make wonderful meals. So let's get cooking.

Other cookery books assume some basic knowledge of cooking techniques, but in this book I have assumed none as I wrote it specifically for the person who knows absolutely *nothing* or *very little* about cooking or meal planning.

The book explains the simple things that one is supposed to know by instinct, such as how to boil an egg or fry sausages, how to prepare and cook vegetables *and* have them ready to eat at the same time as the main course! It includes recipes and suggestions for a variety of snacks and main meals (not all cooked in the frying pan or made from mince), using fish, chicken, beef, lamb, pork and vegetables. The majority of the meals are quick, easy and economical to make, but there is a 'Sunday Lunch' section near the end of the book.

There is also a short section for quick and easy puds and cakes, but it is so easy to be tempted by delicious displays of fresh, chilled and frozen sweets in the supermarkets – look out for the 'Special Offers' if you have a sweet tooth! Remember that yogurt makes a good, cheap sweet and that fresh fruit is the best pud you can eat. Also fruit juice, smoothies or milk is far better for you than fizzy drinks or alcohol.

In many cookery books the recipes are geared for feeding four or more people, but the recipes contained here are designed for the single person living on his or her own (although you can always double the quantity of ingredients if you are cooking with a friend). However, the book does include a few recipes which cater for two people. This is because it is easier to cook larger portions of stews or casseroles as very small amounts tend to dry up during cooking.

REHEATING FOOD

One note of warning: be very careful about reheating cooked food, whether yesterday's leftovers from the fridge or other chilled or frozen dishes. If you must do this, always be sure that the food is re-cooked right through, not merely warmed. *Food just reheated can make you extremely ill if not cooked thoroughly, especially pork and chicken – you have been warned!*

FOLLOWING THE RECIPES

I have given an indication in each recipe of how long it takes to prepare and cook so that, before you start cooking, you will know approximately how much time to set aside for making the meal. Read the recipe right through so that you know what it involves.

The ingredients used in each recipe are all readily available and listed in the order they are used in the method. Collect all the specified ingredients *before* you start cooking, otherwise you may find yourself lacking something vital when you have already prepared half the meal. When the meal is ready, there should be no ingredients left – if there are, you have missed something out!

MEASUREMENTS

The ingredients are given in both metric and imperial measurements. Follow one type of measure or the other, but do not combine the two, as the quantities are not exact conversions.

I have used large or medium free-range eggs in the recipes – the small difference in weight will not affect the end results.

Meat, fish and vegetables can be weighed in the shop when you buy them, or will have the weight on the packet. Don't buy more *fresh* ingredients than you need for the recipe, as extra bits tend to get left at the back of the fridge and wasted. However, it is worthwhile buying some goods in the larger size packets – breakfast cereals, rice, pasta, stock cubes, ketchup, etc, will keep fresh for ages and be on hand when you need them.

In case you don't own kitchen scales, some of the measurements are also given in tea cups (a normal drinking size cup which approximates to 150 ml/5 fl oz/$^1/_4$ pint or half fill a normal drinking mug which will give the same measurement; it isn't the American measuring cup, which is larger), and also in different sized English spoonfuls if appropriate.

ABBREVIATIONS

tsp	= teaspoonful
dsp	= dessertspoonful
tbsp	= tablespoonful
1 spoonful	= 1 slightly rounded spoonful
1 level spoonful	= 1 flat spoonful
1 cupful	= 1 English teacupful or half a normal drinking mug (not the American cup)
g	= gram
kg	= kilogram
oz	= ounce
lb	= pound

SOME HANDY MEASUREMENTS

Butter and Soft Fat Spreads

2.5 cm cube/1 inch cube = 25 g/1 oz; it is easy to divide up a new packet and mark it out in squares.

Cheese

2.5 cm cube/1 inch cube = 25 g/1 oz approximately.

Flour

1 very heaped tbsp = 25 g/1 oz approximately.

Pasta (Shells, Bows, etc)

1 very full cup = 75 g/3 oz approximately.

Rice

$1/_2$ cup dry uncooked rice = 50 g/2 oz approximately

Sugar

1 heaped tbsp = 25 g/1 oz approximately

Sausages

Chipolatas: 8 sausages in a 225 g/8 oz pack.

Thick sausages: 4 sausages in a 225 g/8 oz pack.

AMOUNTS TO USE WHEN COOKING FOR ONE

Minced Beef	100–175 g/4–6 oz
Roast Beef	Approximately 175 g/6 oz per person. A joint weighing 1–1.5 kg/2$^1/_2$–3 lb should serve 6–8 helpings; remember you can enjoy cold meat for sandwiches or dinner the next day
Beef Steak	175–225 g/6–8 oz is a fair sized steak
Chicken	Allow a 175–225 g/6–8 oz chicken joint (leg or breast) per person. A 1–1.5 kg/2$^1/_2$–3 lb chicken serves 3–4 people

Oily Fish	1 whole fish (trout, mackerel, herring) 175–225 g/6–8 oz fillet of salmon, tuna, etc
Smoked Fish: Kippers, Smoked Mackerel Fillets, etc	1–2 fillets according to appetite. Usually sold pre-packed
White Fish	175–225 g/6–8 oz fillet of cod, haddock, etc 1–2 fillets or 1 whole fish (plaice, sole, etc) according to size
Lamb Chops or Lamb Cutlets	1–3 according to size and appetite
Minced Lamb	100–175 g/4–6 oz
Roast Lamb: Leg or Shoulder	1 kg/2$^1/_2$ lb serves 4 people with bone in, or 5–6 people if boned
Pasta Shapes, Spaghetti, Noodles, etc	75g–100 g/3–4 oz/ 1 very generous cup of uncooked pasta
Pork Chops, Pork or Gammon Steaks	1 per person or 175 g/6 oz meat
Roast Pork	Allow 225 g/8 oz per serving. A boneless joint weighing 1.5 kg/2$^1/_2$ lb will give 5–6 generous helpings
Potatoes	225 g/8 oz/ 3–4 potatoes according to size and appetite

Rice	50–75 g/2–3 oz/ $^1/_2$–$^3/_4$ cup dry uncooked rice
Stewing Steak	100–175 g/4–6 oz
Vegetables	See the individual vegetables in section 4.

USING THE OVEN

Temperatures are given for both electric and gas ovens. Remember always to heat the oven for a few minutes before putting food in it, so that the whole of the oven reaches the appropriate temperature before the food is added.

KITCHEN EQUIPMENT

This section may be particularly useful if you're a student or are living away from home and cooking for yourself for the first time in your life. Some accommodation may provide everything you need, while in other places you may have to start from scratch and find everything for yourself. Check through the items listed below and try to buy, beg or 'borrow' from home what you think you will need before you move in, adding or replacing items through the year as necessary.

Baking tin for meat or vegetables
Baking tins (various) for cakes, buns or Yorkshire puds
Basins (various)
Blender
Bottle opener
Bread bin or crock
Cake tin or plastic container to store cake and biscuits, etc
Chopping/bread board

Cling film

Colander

Cooking foil

Foil dishes (these are cheap and last for several bakings; useful if you need a tin of a particular shape or size)

Frying pan

Grater

Kettle – electric or stove-top type

Kitchen paper

Kitchen scissors

Kitchen tools: draining spoon, ladle, spatula, potato masher, slice, whisk

Knives: bread knife with serrated edge, sharp chopping knife for meat, vegetable knife

Measuring jug for liquids (can also be used as a basin)

Oven proof dishes (pyrex type)

Plastic storage containers for flour, rice, pasta, etc

Rolling pin

Saucepans

Sieve

Spoons (tablespoon, dessertspoon, teaspoon)

Storage jars for sugar, etc

Tin opener

Toaster

Toastie bags – use in the toaster to make toasted sandwiches

Wooden spoons

Microwave oven – really useful, either just a microwave or a multi-purpose cooker. Handy when cooking or heating small amounts for one person, and a great addition in a shared house where several people may be trying to cook at the same time.

STORES TO STOCK YOUR NEW KITCHEN

Dried goods (they keep for ages, just check the 'use by' date

Coffee (ground)	Mustard
Coffee (instant)	Pasta (dried)
Couscous	Pepper
Curry powder or paste	Rice (long grain)
Dried herbs	Salt
Drinking chocolate	Stock cubes
Flour	Sugar
Gravy granules	Tea bags

Oils, Sauces, Preserves, Spreads, etc

Chocolate spread/Nutella	Marmite
Cooking oil	Olive oil
Fruit squash	Peanut butter
Golden syrup	Pickle or chutney
Honey	Salad cream/dressings
Horseradish sauce	Soy sauce
Hot pepper sauce/Tabasco	Tomato ketchup
HP/Brown sauce	Vinegar
Jam/Marmalade	Worcester sauce

Handy tins and packs for a quick meal/pudding

Baked beans	Corned beef
Beans with sausages	Custard
Beef casserole	Frankfurter sausages
Chicken in sauce	Instant whip
Chick peas	Italian tomatoes
'Cook-in' sauces (add meat and/or veg for a quick pasta sauce/casserole)	Jellies
	Luncheon meat
	Lentils

Minced beef in sauce
Mushy peas
Fresh pasta sauces (cheese,
    tomato, etc, sold in cartons
    in the chiller cabinet, ready
    to cook with pasta, etc)
Pot noodles
Red kidney beans

Rice pudding
Sardines
Soups
Spaghetti
Spaghetti hoops
Sweetcorn
Tinned fruit
Tuna fish

Perishable foods (these don't last long but are useful to have as a 'starter' pack)

Bacon
Biscuits
Bread
Breakfast cereals
Butter/spread
Cheese
Cooked meats

Eggs
Fresh fruit
Fruit juice
Soft dried fruit
Fresh milk
Porridge oats
Potatoes

'Short cut' foods to buy ready made

Frozen chips	Cook in the oven, grill or microwave
Pastry	Short crust or flaky, fresh or frozen
Pizza	Fresh or frozen – add extra toppings
Mixed salad leaves	Good varieties, sold in bags ready to use

Store sugar, flour, pasta, rice, biscuits, cake, etc, in airtight containers rather than leaving them in open packets on the shelf. This keeps them fresh and clean for much longer and protects them from ants and other insects. If kitchen space is short, in a shared kitchen, buy a large plastic container in which several opened packets can be stored.

Also don't forget you'll need washing up liquid, washing up brush, tea towels, j-cloths, oven gloves, pan scrubber, multi-purpose cleaner for sinks and cookers, and surface spray for worktops.

COOKING TERMS EXPLAINED

Al dente
Refers to pasta that is cooked and feels firm when bitten.

Baking
Cooking food, usually cakes, pastry, biscuits or ready prepared dishes, in a hot or moderate oven.

Basting
Spooning fat or butter or meat juices over food that is being roasted (particularly meat and poultry) to keep it moist.

Beating
Mixing food with a wooden spoon or whisk so that the lumps disappear and it becomes smooth.

Binding
Adding eggs, cream or butter to a dry mixture to hold it together.

Blending
Mixing dry ingredients (such as flour) with a little liquid to make a runny lump-free mixture.

Boiling
Cooking food in boiling water (at a temperature of 100°C/ 212°F) with the water bubbling gently.

Boning
Removing the bones from meat, poultry or fish.

Braising
Frying meat in hot fat so that it is just browned, and then cooking it slowly in a covered dish or pan with a little liquid and some vegetables, either in the oven or on top of the stove.

Casserole
An ovenproof or flameproof dish with a lid. Also an oven cooked stew.

Chilling
Cooling food in a fridge without freezing.

Colander
A perforated metal or plastic basket used for straining food.

Deep-frying
Immersing food in hot fat or oil and frying it – you need a deep fat fryer, preferably an electric pan with a thermostat, for this.

Dicing
Cutting food into small cubes.

Dot with butter
Cover food with small pieces of butter before baking or grilling.

Flaking
Separating fish into flaky pieces, usually after cooking.

Frying
Cooking food in oil or fat in a pan (usually a flat frying pan).

Greasing a dish
Smearing butter, fat or a little cooking oil on the inside of a dish to prevent the ingredients sticking to it while cooking.

Grilling
Cooking or browning food by direct heat under a grill.

Mixing
Combining ingredients by stirring with a spoon or fork.

Nest (making a)
Arranging food (such as rice or creamed potato) around a serving plate to make a circular border, and arranging other food into the middle of this 'nest'.

Poaching
Cooking food in water or sugar syrup which is just below boiling point.

Purée
Food that has been passed through a sieve and reduced to a pulp, or pulped in a food processor or blender.

Roasting
Cooking food, usually meat or vegetables, in a little fat in a hot oven.

Sautéing
Frying food quickly in a little hot fat, and turning it frequently in the pan so that it browns quickly.

Seasoning
Adding salt, pepper, herbs and/or spices to food.

Simmering
Cooking food in water which is just below boiling point so that only an occasional bubble appears.

Straining
Separating solid food from liquid by draining it through a sieve or colander, e.g. potatoes, peas, broccoli, etc, that have been cooked in boiling water.

1
EGGS

Eggs are super value, quick to cook and can make a snack or main meal in minutes. If you have eggs in the fridge, you can always produce breakfast, lunch, tea or dinner at a moment's notice. In fact, when we lived in a rather remote part of the Middle East, one of my neighbours asserted that as long as she had a tray of fresh eggs in the house she knew that her family would never starve – what better recommendation could you ask for than that!

Eggs can be cooked in so many different ways that most people will enjoy an egg – unless they suffer from an egg allergy of course – but you may have to cook eggs a different way for each friend or member of the family!

In view of the occasional scares over salmonella in eggs, take care about the eggs you buy and store them sensibly and hygienically. Eggs have porous shells and should never be stored where they are in contact with uncooked meat or fish, dust or dirt of any kind. They also absorb smells through the shells, so be aware if you are buying soap, washing powder, household cleaners, firelighters, etc, and keep them in separate shopping bags.

Heed the advice on fresh eggs given out by the health authorities: only buy eggs from a reputable supplier and *do not serve raw or lightly cooked eggs, homemade mayonnaise, sweet or savoury mousse or other dishes containing uncooked eggs to babies, pregnant women, the elderly or anyone following a course of chemotherapy or other treatment that may affect their immune system.* Don't panic, but just take reasonable care with egg cookery and enjoy all the delicious dishes you can make with eggs.

BOILED EGG

Use an egg already at room temperature if possible, not one straight from the fridge as otherwise it may crack. If you prick the top of the shell once with a special gadget or a clean pin, the egg will not crack while cooking. (My daughter-in-law Barbara taught me this, and it really does work.)

Slip the egg carefully into a small saucepan, cover with warm (not boiling) water and add $1/2$ tsp salt (to seal up any cracks). Bring to the boil, note the time and turn down the heat before the egg starts rattling about in the pan. Simmer gently, timing from when the water begins to boil, using the table below:

Size	Time	Description
Large/Medium	3 mins	soft-boiled
Large/Medium	4 mins	soft yolk, hard white
Large/Medium	10 mins	hard-boiled

SOFT-BOILED

Remove carefully from the pan with a spoon, put into an egg cup and tap the top to crack the shell to stop the egg continuing to cook inside.

HARD-BOILED

Remove the pan from the heat and place under cold, running water to prevent a black ring forming round the yolk. Peel off shell and rinse in cold water to remove any shell still clinging to the egg.

POACHED EGG

Put about 2.5 cm (1 inch) water into a clean frying pan and bring to the boil. Reduce the heat so that the water is just simmering.

Crack the egg carefully into a cup or mug, and slide it into the simmering water. Cook very gently, just simmering in the hot water, for about 3 minutes, until the egg is set to your liking.

Lift it out with a slotted spoon or fish slice, being careful not to break the yolk underneath.

HOW TO SEPARATE AN EGG

METHOD 1
Have two cups or basins ready. Crack the egg carefully, and pull the two halves apart, letting the white drain into one basin, and keeping the yolk in the shell, until all the white has drained out. Tip the yolk into the other basin. If the yolk breaks, tip the whole lot into another basin and start again with another egg.

METHOD 2
Carefully break the egg and tip it onto a saucer, making sure the yolk is not broken. Place a glass over the yolk, and gently tip the white into a basin, keeping the yolk on the saucer with the glass.

FRIED EGG

Heat a small amount of cooking oil, butter or dripping in a frying pan over a moderate heat (not too hot, or the egg white will frazzle).

Carefully break the egg into a cup to check that it is not bad, then pour it into the frying pan and fry gently for 2–3 minutes.

To cook the top of the egg, either baste the egg occasionally by spooning a little of the hot fat over it, or put the lid on the pan and let the heat cook it.

You may prefer the egg carefully flipped over when half done to cook on both sides, but be prepared for a broken yolk.

Remove the egg from the pan with a fish slice or wide-bladed knife.

FRIED BREAD

A deliciously wicked accompaniment to fried eggs as well as with a big cooked breakfast.

Takes 4–5 minutes

1–2 tsp cooking oil (olive oil tastes good)
Knob of butter
1–2 slices of bread

Put the oil and butter into a frying pan over a moderate heat. When the fat is hot (but not smoking or the oil will burn), slide in the bread and fry for 1–2 minutes on each side, adding a little more butter to the pan if necessary.

SCRAMBLED EGGS

Usually you will want to scramble two or more eggs at a time.

Chopped chives are tasty with scrambled eggs. Simply wash them, cut off their roots and chop them.

Beat the egg well with a fork in a basin or large cup. Add salt, pepper and chopped chives.

Melt a large knob of butter in a small, preferably thick, saucepan. Turn the heat to low and pour in the beaten egg, stirring all the time, until the egg looks thick and creamy. Do not overcook, as the egg will continue to cook even when removed from the heat.

Stir in (if required) 1–2 tsp cream or top of the milk, or a small knob of butter (this helps to stop the egg cooking any more).

CHEESY SCRAMBLED EGGS
Add 25 g/1 oz grated or crumbled Cheddar cheese to the beaten eggs before cooking.

PAN SCRAMBLE
If you are cooking sausages or bacon as well as scrambled eggs, fry the meat first and then cook the eggs in the same hot fat.

PIPERADE

Serves 1

Scrambled eggs plus a bit extra. Eat with hot buttered toast or crusty fresh bread rolls.

Takes 30 minutes

1 small onion
Small green pepper
2 tomatoes (fresh or tinned)
1 tbsp oil or knob of butter (for frying)
Pinch of garlic powder
Salt and pepper
2–3 eggs

Peel and slice the onion. Wash, core and chop the green pepper. Wash and chop the fresh tomatoes or drain the tinned tomatoes and chop roughly.

Heat the butter or oil in a saucepan. Cook the onion and pepper over a medium heat, stirring well, until soft (about 5 minutes).

Add the chopped tomatoes, garlic, salt and pepper, and stir. Put a lid on the pan and continue to cook gently over a low heat, stirring occasionally, for about 15–20 minutes, to make a thick saucy mixture.

Break the eggs into a small basin or large cup. Lightly beat them with a fork, then pour them into the vegetable mixture, stirring hard with a wooden spoon, until the eggs are just setting. Pour onto a warm plate and serve.

SAVOURY EGGS

A cheap and tasty variation on the bacon 'n egg theme. It makes a good, quick supper.

For a change, cooked sliced sausages or slices of salami can be used instead of bacon.

Takes 25 minutes

1 small onion
1 small eating apple
1 rasher of bacon
2 tsp cooking oil or large knob of butter (for frying)
Salt and pepper
$1/_4$ tsp sugar
2 eggs

Peel and slice the onion. Wash, core and slice the apple. De-rind the bacon and cut into 1.25 cm/$^1/_2$ inch pieces.

Heat the oil or butter in a frying pan over a moderate heat. Add the bacon, onion and apple, and fry, stirring occasionally, until soft (about 5 minutes). Stir in the salt, pepper and sugar.

Remove from the heat. Break the eggs into a cup, one at a time, and pour on top of the onion mixture. Cover the pan with a lid and cook for a further 3–5 minutes over a very low heat, until the eggs are as firm as you like them.

CHEESY BAKED EGG

Serves 1

Quite delicious, and so easy to make. Serve with crusty French bread, rolls or crisp toast and a salad.

Takes 20 minutes

75–100 g/3–4 oz Cheddar or other hard cheese
2 eggs
Salt and pepper
Large knob of butter

Heat the oven at 180°C/350°F/Fan 160°C/Gas Mark 4. Grease an ovenproof dish well with some butter.

Grate the cheese and cover the base of the dish with half of the cheese.

Break the eggs, one a time, into a cup, then slide them carefully on top of the cheese. Season well with the salt and pepper, and cover the eggs completely with the rest of the cheese.

Dot with the butter and bake in the hot oven for about 15 minutes, until the cheese is bubbling and the eggs are just set.

EGG NESTS

These can be served plain, or with the addition of grated cheese, or with a fresh tomato or salad, to make a very cheap lunch or supper.

Takes 30 minutes

2–4 potatoes
Large knob of butter
50 g/2 oz Cheddar cheese (optional)
Salt and pepper
2 eggs

Peel the potatoes, cut into thick slices and cook in boiling water in a saucepan for 10–15 minutes, until soft.

Drain and mash with a fork, then beat in the large knob of butter, using a wooden spoon. Grate the cheese (if using) and beat half of it into the potato. Season with the salt and pepper.

Grease an ovenproof dish. Spread the potato into this and make a nest for the eggs. Keep it warm.

Boil 2.5 cm/1 inch water in a clean frying pan and poach the eggs. If making cheesy eggs, heat the grill.

Carefully lift the eggs out of the water when cooked and put them into the potato nest. If making plain eggs, serve at once, otherwise cover the eggs with the remainder of the grated cheese and brown for a few moments under the hot grill.

SICILIAN EGGS

Serves 1

Saucy tomatoes with eggs and bacon. Serve with hot toast.

Takes 25 minutes

2 eggs
1 small onion
Knob of butter
1 small (230 g/8 oz) tin of tomatoes
Salt and pepper
Pinch of sugar
Pinch of dried herbs
2 rashers of bacon (de-rinded)

Hard boil the eggs for 10 minutes. Cool them in cold, running water. Shell them, rinse clean, slice thickly and arrange in a greased, heatproof dish.

Peel and slice the onion. Fry it in the butter in a small saucepan over a moderate heat until soft (about 5 minutes).

Add the tomatoes, salt, pepper, sugar and herbs. Cook gently for a further 5 minutes. Heat the grill.

Pour the tomato mixture over the eggs, top with the de-rinded bacon rashers and place under the hot grill until the bacon is cooked.

> **QUICK TIP** *If you don't have a grill, fry the bacon in the pan with the onions, remove it and keep it hot while the tomatoes are cooking, then top the tomato mixture with the hot, cooked bacon.*

EGG, CHEESE AND ONION SAVOURY

Serves 1

Cheap and cheerful, eaten with chunks of hot, crusty bread.

Takes 30 minutes

2 eggs
1 onion
Knob of butter (for frying)
25 g/1 oz grated Cheddar cheese (for the topping)

For the cheese sauce (or just use grated cheese or packet sauce mix)
2 tsp flour
150 ml/$^1/_4$ pint/1 cup milk
12 g/$^1/_2$ oz butter
25 g/1 oz grated Cheddar cheese
Salt and pepper
Pinch of mustard

Hard boil the eggs for 10 minutes. Peel and slice the onion and fry gently in the knob of butter in a small saucepan over a moderate heat, for 4–5 minutes, until soft and cooked.

For the cheese sauce, mix the flour into a smooth paste with a little of the milk in a small basin. Boil the rest of the milk and pour onto the flour mixture, stirring all the time. Then pour the whole mixture back into the saucepan and stir over the heat until the mixture thickens. Stir in the butter and beat well. Add the cheese, salt, pepper and mustard.

Put the onion into a greased ovenproof dish. Slice the cold, hardboiled eggs and arrange on top of the onion. Cover with the cheese sauce and sprinkle with the rest of the grated cheese. Brown under a hot grill for a few minutes, until the cheese is melted, crisp and bubbly.

EGGY BREAD OR FRENCH TOAST

Serves 1

A boarding school favourite.

Serve with golden syrup, honey or jam, or sprinkled with white or brown sugar.

Or to make it savoury, sprinkle with salt, pepper and a blob of tomato sauce. Savoury eggy bread goes well with bacon, sausages and baked beans.

Takes 15 minutes

1 egg
1–2 tsp sugar (according to taste)
75 ml/$2^1/_2$ fl oz/$^1/_2$ cup milk
3–4 thick slices of white bread
50 g/2 oz butter (for frying)

Beat the egg in a basin or a large cup. Add the sugar and beat well with a whisk, mixer or fork, gradually adding the milk. Pour this egg mixture into a shallow dish or soup plate, and soak each slice of bread in the egg, until it is all soaked up.

Heat a frying pan over a moderate heat. Melt the butter in the pan and fry the soaked bread slices in the hot butter, turning to cook both sides, until golden brown and crispy.

Serve at once as above.

FRENCH OMELETTE

Serves 1

Light golden egg, folded over into an envelope shape, served plain or with a wide variety of sweet or savoury fillings. French bread, bread rolls, sauté or new potatoes, a side salad or just fresh tomatoes make delicious accompaniments. There's no need for a special omelette pan (unless you happen to own one, of course). Use any clean, ordinary frying pan.

Takes 10 minutes

2–3 eggs
1 tsp cold water per egg
Pinch of salt and pepper (omit for sweet omelettes)
Knob of butter
Filling as required

Prepare the filling (see opposite). Warm a plate. Break the eggs into a basin or large cup, add the water, salt and pepper and beat with a fork.

Put the butter in a frying pan, heat over a moderate heat until it is just sizzling (but not brown), and pour the egg mixture in the pan at once. Carefully, with a wide-bladed knife or wooden spoon, draw the mixture from the middle to the sides of the pan, so that the uncooked egg in the middle can run onto the hot pan and set. Continue until all the egg is very lightly cooked underneath and the top is still running and soft (about one minute). The top will cook in its own heat when it is folded over.

With a wide-bladed knife or a fish slice, loosen the omelette so that you can remove it easily from the pan. Put the filling across the middle of the omelette and fold both sides over it to make an envelope. If using a cold filling, cook for a further minute. Remove from the pan, place on the warm plate and serve at once.

OMELETTE AND PANCAKE FILLINGS

For pancakes, see page 238.

Savoury

Asparagus

Use $^1/_2$ small (298 g) can asparagus tips. Heat them through in a small saucepan. Drain and keep hot. Or use fresh asparagus, lightly cooked – see page 76.

Bacon

Fry 1–2 rashers of bacon in a little oil or fat. Keep hot.

Cheese

25–50 g/1–2 oz grated or finely cubed cheese.

Chicken

2–3 tbsp chopped, cooked chicken. (You can use the pickings from a roast chicken.)

Fresh or Dried Herbs

Add 1 tsp chopped fresh herbs or 2 tsp dried herbs to the beaten egg mixture. Choose herbs according to taste.

Cooked Meat

Chop 1–2 slices cooked ham, salami or garlic sausage, etc.

Mushrooms

Wash and chop 50 g/2 oz/4–5 mushrooms. Cook gently in a small pan, with a knob of butter, for 2–3 minutes, stirring occasionally. Keep hot.

Tomato

Wash 1–2 tomatoes, slice and fry them in a little oil or fat and keep hot.

Sweet

Choose one of the following fillings, then sprinkle the omelettes or pancakes with 1 tsp icing or granulated sugar, just before serving.

Chocolate
Add 1–2 dsp chocolate spread or Nutella. Sprinkle the top with a little drinking chocolate.

Fruit
Add 2–3 tbsp sliced, tinned fruit (peaches, pineapple or apricot) or 2–3 tbsp sliced fresh fruit (bananas, peaches, strawberries or raspberries).

Honey
Add 2–3 tbsp honey.

Honey and Walnut
Use 2–3 tbsp honey, 1 tbsp chopped walnuts.

Jam
Add 1–2 tbsp jam or bramble jelly. Warm the jam by standing it in a saucepan with 5 cm/2 inches hot water, and warming gently over a low heat before spooning over the omelette or pancake.

Marmalade
Add 2–3 tbsp orange or ginger marmalade – warm as above to make the marmalade easier to spread.

Sugar and Lemon – more traditionally used with pancakes
Sprinkle with 1–2 tsp granulated sugar and a good squeeze of lemon juice.

EGG MAYONNAISE SALAD

Serves 1 main meal or 2 starters

A delicious summer salad. Serve with new potatoes and/or bread rolls or garlic bread as a main course, and bread rolls or bread and butter as a starter.

Takes 20 minutes

2 fresh eggs
1 mixed green salad (see page 62)
2 tbsp mayonnaise
1–2 tsp salad dressing
Pinch of ground paprika pepper

Hard boil the eggs (see page 23). While the eggs are cooking, prepare the green salad (see page 62), adding extra salad vegetables if liked, and arrange on a serving plate. Shell, wash and dry the cooked eggs, cut in half lengthways and place in the middle of the salad. Spoon the mayonnaise over the eggs. Just before serving, pour a little dressing over the salad leaves and sprinkle a pinch of paprika on top of the mayonnaise.

EGG AND PRAWN MAYONNAISE
Add 25–50 g/1–2 oz cooked shelled prawns and scatter them on top of the salad, around the eggs.

PRAWN MAYONNAISE/MARIE ROSE
Just use 1 hardboiled egg
Add 50–75 g/2–3 oz cooked shelled prawns
$^1/_2$ tsp tomato ketchup

Slice the prepared hardboiled egg and arrange around the plate on top of the salad. Pile the prawns in the middle of the salad. Mix the ketchup into the mayonnaise to make Sauce Marie Rose, and spoon on top of the prawns.

SPANISH OMELETTE

Serves 1

A delicious, filling, savoury omelette. Served flat like a thick pancake, mixed with onion, potato, cooked meat and other vegetables, it's a good way of using up cold, cooked leftovers. (A large omelette, made with four eggs and some extra vegetables, can be cut in half, serving two people.)

Takes 15 minutes

Extras (optional)
**Bacon: 1–2 rashers of bacon, chopped and fried
   with the onion
Cooked meat: 1–2 slices of chopped, cooked ham,
   salami or garlic sausage, etc
Green peppers: 1–2 tbsp green peppers, chopped
   and mixed with the onion
Sausages: 1–2 cold, cooked sausages, sliced
Vegetables: 1–2 tbsp cold cooked vegetables (peas,
   sweetcorn, green beans, mixed vegetables)**

**1 small onion
2–3 boiled potatoes
2–3 eggs
1 tsp cold water per egg
Salt and pepper
Pinch of dried herbs (optional)
1 tbsp oil (for frying)**

Prepare the 'extras' if used. Peel and chop the onion. Dice the cooked potatoes. Beat the eggs, water, seasoning and herbs lightly with a fork in a small basin.

Heat the oil in an omelette or frying pan over a medium heat, and fry the onion for 3–5 minutes, until soft.

Add the diced potato and continue frying until the potato is thoroughly heated. Add the extra meat or vegetables (if using) and heat through again.

Heat the grill and warm a plate.

Pour the beaten egg mixture into the pan, over the vegetables, and cook without stirring until the bottom is firm, but with the top remaining creamy and moist (about 1–2 minutes). Shake the pan occasionally to prevent sticking.

Place under the hot grill for 30 seconds, until the top is set – beware in case the pan handle gets hot. Slide the omelette flat onto the warm plate and serve at once.

DRINKING EGG OR EGG NOG

Serves 1

A nourishing breakfast for those in a hurry, or an easily-digested meal for those feeling fragile!

Takes 5 minutes

1 egg
2 tsp sugar
300 ml/$^1/_2$ pint/2 cups milk (cold or warm)
2 tsp brandy, rum or whisky (optional but not for breakfast! or 1 tbsp sherry (optional but, again, not for breakfast!)
Pinch of nutmeg or cinnamon

Break the egg into a basin, beat it lightly with a mixer, egg whisk or fork, adding the sugar and gradually beating in the milk. Add the spirits (if used). Pour into a tall glass, sprinkle nutmeg or cinnamon on top and serve at once.

This dish is unsuitable for babies and young children, pregnant women, the elderly or anyone with a poor immune system, as the egg is served raw.

2
CHEESE

If you like cheese, you'll enjoy these delicious meals and snacks using different cheeses. They're cheap and quick to make too. Any tasty hard-type cheese can be used instead of Cheddar, or use a nice strong Blue Cheese (crumbled instead of grated), sliced Brie, Camembert, Mozzarella or any of your favourite cheeses. Strong cheeses give more flavour when used in cooking.

There are more recipes using cheese in sections 4 and 5.

EASY WELSH RAREBIT
(CHEESE ON TOAST)

Serves 1

This is the quickest method of making cheese on toast. It can be served plain, or topped with pickle or chutney, sliced tomato or crispy, cooked bacon.

Takes 5–10 minutes

1–3 rashers of bacon (optional)
1–2 tomatoes (optional)
50–75 g/2–3 oz/2–3 slices Cheddar, Brie or Blue cheese
2–3 slices of bread (white or brown)
Butter (for spreading)
1 tbsp pickle or chutney (optional)

Heat the grill. Lightly grill the bacon, if used.

Slice the tomatoes, if used. Slice the cheese, making enough slices to cover the pieces of bread.

Toast the bread lightly on both sides and spread one side with the butter. Arrange the slices of cheese on the buttered side of the toast and put under the grill for 1–2 minutes, until the cheese begins to bubble.

Top with the tomato slices, bacon or pickle/chutney and return to the grill for another minute, to heat the topping and brown the cheese. Eat at once.

TRADITIONAL WELSH RAREBIT

Serves 1

More soft and creamy than cheese on toast, and only takes a few more minutes to prepare.

Takes 10 minutes

1–3 rashers of bacon (optional)
1–2 tomatoes (optional)
50–75 g/2–3 oz cheese
1 tsp milk
Pinch of mustard
Shake of pepper
1 tbsp pickle or chutney (optional)
2–3 slices of bread and butter

Heat the grill. Lightly grill the bacon, if used. Slice the tomatoes, if used.

Grate the cheese and mix into a stiff paste with the milk in a bowl, stirring in the mustard and pepper.

Lightly toast the bread, and spread one side with the butter, then generously cover it with the cheese mixture.

Put under the hot grill for 1–2 minutes, until the cheese starts to bubble. Top with the bacon, tomato slices or pickle or chutney, and return to the grill for another minute, to heat the topping and brown the cheese.

Serve at once.

BUCK RAREBIT

Serves 1

Welsh Rarebit with poached eggs. When the toast is covered with the cheese, and ready to pop back under the grill to brown, prepare one or two poached eggs by cooking them gently in simmering water for 2–3 minutes. See page 24.

While the eggs are cooking, put the toast and cheese slices under the grill to brown. When they are golden and bubbling, and the eggs are cooked, carefully remove the eggs from the water and slide them onto the hot, cheesy toast. Serve immediately.

BOOZY WELSH RAREBIT

Serves 1

Open a can of beer, use a little in the cooking, and drink the rest with your meal.

Takes 10–15 minutes

50–75 g/2–3 oz cheese
Knob of butter
1–2 tsp beer
Shake of pepper
Pinch of mustard
1–2 slices of bread (white or brown)

Grate the cheese and heat the grill.

Melt the butter in a small saucepan over a moderate heat. Add the cheese, beer, pepper and mustard, and stir well over the heat, until the cheese begins to melt, and the mixture begins to boil. Remove the saucepan from the heat.

Toast the bread lightly on both sides. Carefully pour the cheese mixture onto the toast, and put back under the grill for a few moments, until the cheese is hot, bubbling and golden brown.

Serve at once – delicious!

CHEESY FRANKFURTER TOASTS

Serves 1

A quick snack, made with food from the store cupboard.

Takes 15 minutes

2–3 slices of bread
12 g/$^1/_2$ oz butter
2–3 slices of cooked ham, garlic sausage
**   or luncheon meat (optional)**
Small can (227 g/8 oz; actual weight of sausages
**   163 g/4 oz) Frankfurter sausages**
2–3 slices of cheese (pre-packed slices are ideal)

Heat the grill. Lightly toast the bread on one side.

Butter the untoasted side of the bread. Lay the ham or garlic sausage on the untoasted side and top with the Frankfurters.

Cover with the cheese slices, and cook under the hot grill until the cheese has melted. Eat at once.

> **QUICK TIP** *If you don't have a grill, the bread can be heated in a hot oven (200°C/400°F/Fan 180°C/Gas Mark 6) for a few minutes, and then buttered. Place the 'toast' with the topping back into the oven, on an ovenproof dish, and cook for 5–10 minutes, until the cheese has melted.*

CHEESE FONDUE

Serves 2

Use a fondue set if you have one, or a small, heavy saucepan. The fondue is cooked over a low heat on the stove and then taken to the table. Cheese fondue works well without a burner as it does not need to be kept boiling like an oil fondue for meat or vegetables.

You can substitute the Gruyère or Emmenthal cheese with Cheddar or other hard cheeses which will be cheaper. For a non-alcoholic fondue, use apple juice instead of wine or cider. Ordinary forks can be used instead of fondue forks.

Takes 20 minutes

1 small French stick
1 clove of fresh garlic
2 tsp flour
150 ml/$^1/_4$ pint/1 cup dry white wine or cider
100 g/4 oz Gruyère cheese, grated
100 g/4 oz Emmenthal cheese, grated
Black pepper

Cut the French stick into bite-sized chunks and put into a serving bowl.

Peel and halve the garlic clove and crush it round the base and sides of the fondue pot or saucepan. Discard the garlic pieces.

Put the flour into a basin or cup, and mix to a smooth, runny paste with 2 tbsp of the wine or cider.

Pour the remaining wine or cider into the fondue pot/saucepan over a low heat, gradually stirring in the grated cheese with a wooden spoon, stirring until the cheese has melted. Remove from the heat.

Stir the flour mixture again and stir it into the fondue. Put the pot back over the heat and stir the fondue well until the mixture is thick, smooth and just bubbling. Season with black pepper.

Carefully carry the hot fondue pot to the table and place on the burner (if you have one) over a low flame, or stand the hot pan on a thick table mat and reheat on the cooker if necessary.

Always use the correct fuel recommended for your fondue set, and put the burner in place before lighting it. NEVER CARRY A LIGHTED BURNER ACROSS THE KITCHEN TO THE TABLE!

CAULIFLOWER CHEESE

Serves 1

Filling enough for a supper dish with crusty French bread and butter, or serve as a vegetable dish with meat or fish.

Takes 30 minutes

1 portion (3–4 florets) cauliflower
1 slice of bread (crumbled or grated into crumbs)
Knob of butter
1 sliced tomato (optional)

For the cheese sauce (or just use 50 g/2 oz grated cheese or packet sauce mix)
50 g/2 oz cheese
2 tsp flour
150 ml/¹/₄ pint/1 cup milk
12 g/¹/₂ oz butter or margarine
Salt and pepper
Pinch of mustard

Trim the cauliflower's stalk, divide it into florets and wash thoroughly. Cook it in boiling water for 5 minutes, until just tender. Drain well.

Make the cheese sauce (see page 228).

Put the cauliflower into a greased ovenproof dish. Cover with the cheese sauce, sprinkle the breadcrumbs on top and add a knob of butter and the tomato slices. Place under a hot grill for a few minutes until golden-brown and crispy.

QUICK TIP *If you don't have time to make the cheese sauce, cover the cauliflower with 50 g/2 oz grated cheese and grill as above.*

3

SOUPS, SANDWICHES, SNACKS AND SALADS

Here are lots of ideas and suggestions for light lunches and suppers with soups, sandwiches and sandwich fillings, packed lunches, hot snacks and lovely fresh, healthy salads which can make a light meal by themselves. Of course, there are plenty of other ideas and recipes throughout the book.

I know it's very easy to buy lunchtime sandwiches and snacks, but if you're on a tight budget you may be surprised how much you can save by making your own sandwich or salad – and of course you don't have to queue up in the rain at the sandwich shop at lunch time!

SOUPS

You can buy the most wonderful selection of ready prepared soups – long-lasting in packets and cans or freshly made and sold in cartons. However, it is fun to make your own sometimes, and you can always use up leftover vegetables, both cooked and raw, by choosing a tasty selection and simmering them in stock (made with a stock cube) until soft, then puréeing to make a smooth soup, or leaving as it is for a chunky soup.

FRENCH ONION SOUP

Serves 2

A lovely thick warming soup, served with a bubbling hot cheese croûton on the top, and lots of extra grated cheese.

Takes about 1$^1/_2$ hours

2 big onions
1 clove garlic or $^1/_2$ tsp garlic powder or garlic paste
2 tbsp cooking oil
Large knob of butter or spread
$^1/_2$ tsp white sugar
150 ml/$^1/_4$ pint white wine (or use red wine if you prefer)
1 vegetable stock cube or 2 tsp stock powder
600 ml/1 pint hot water
Salt and black pepper to taste
2 dsp brandy (optional!)

Topping
2 thick slices of French bread, cut diagonally
100 g/4 oz grated Gruyère or strong Cheddar cheese

Peel and thinly slice the onions. Peel and squash the fresh garlic.

Heat the oil and butter in a medium saucepan, add the onion and garlic (fresh, powder or paste), and fry over a gentle heat, stirring in the sugar. Continue to fry very gently for 15–20 minutes, stirring occasionally, until the onions are soft and a pale golden brown.

Stir in the wine. (If you prefer not to use alcohol, add extra stock.) Dissolve the stock cube or powder in the hot water and add to the onion mixture.

Stir well and simmer for 45–60 minutes over a very low heat. Season with salt and pepper, and add the brandy if you wish.

Prepare croûtons
Heat the grill, then lower the heat and toast the croûtons very slowly so that they dry off and become hard, crispy and very light brown – this will take 5–10 minutes.

When the soup is ready, turn the grill to high. Butter the croûtons, cover thickly with the grated cheese, and toast under the hot grill until the cheese is bubbling and golden. Ladle the soup into deep soup bowls and carefully top each bowlful with a hot cheese croûton. Serve at once with extra cheese and slices of crusty bread.

If you are eating alone, save the extra soup in the fridge or freeze for later.

THICK LEEK AND POTATO SOUP

3–4 generous helpings

Celebrate St David's Day with friends and serve this tasty soup with hot garlic bread, French bread or warm bread rolls, followed by a cheese board of Welsh cheeses (check out the cheese counter at the supermarket or local deli, there are lots of lovely cheeses to try), and eat them with a variety of savoury biscuits and butter, and some sugary Welsh cakes.

Takes about 1 hour

Halve these ingredients if just cooking for one
2–3 leeks (according to size)
2 medium onions
4 medium potatoes
50 g/2 oz butter or spread
2 vegetable stock cubes or 4 tsp stock powder
1.5 litres/2$^{1}/_{2}$ pints water
1 tbsp crème fraîche or double cream
A few fresh chives or sprigs parsley if available

Prepare the leeks and cut into thin rings (see page 88). Peel and finely chop the onions. Peel and dice the potatoes.

Melt the butter or spread in a large saucepan over a gentle heat, add the vegetables, stir well and leave to soften very gently for a few minutes – do not let the vegetables brown.

Put the stock cubes or powder into a measuring jug and dissolve in a little hot water. Pour the stock into the saucepan, add the rest of the hot water, stir well until the soup begins to simmer, then cook gently for 15–20 minutes until the vegetables are soft.

Remove from the heat and purée in a liquidizer or with a blender. (If you don't have a blender, the soup will still taste very good, but will just not be as smooth.) Return the soup to the pan and reheat gently, then ladle into soup bowls, pour the crème fraîche or cream on top and sprinkle with some snipped chives or parsley if available.

SANDWICHES FOR PACKED LUNCHES

Try and ring the changes with different kinds of bread – white, brown, granary, sliced, crusty rolls, soft baps, French bread, ciabatta and pitta bread are a few suggestions. Crisp breads make a change too.

Butter the bread lightly; this stops it going soggy if the filling is moist, and holds the filling in place. (Have you ever tried eating unbuttered egg sandwiches?) Wrap the sandwiches in cling film to keep them fresh – it's worth buying a roll if you take sandwiches often – or put them into a polythene bag. A plastic container will stop them getting squashed.

Lettuce, tomato, cucumber, celery and green peppers are a good addition, either sliced in the sandwiches or eaten separately, with them. Treat yourself to some fresh fruit as well, according to what is in season.

Avocado
Halve the avocado, remove the stone and spoon the inside into a basin. Mash with a fork, adding 1–2 tbsp mayonnaise to make a spread.

BLT
A firm favourite in sandwich shops and pubs, but why not make your own just as you like it?

Trim excess fat off the bacon. Wash and dry some crisp fresh lettuce and slice one or two large tomatoes. Fry the bacon, adding the tomato slices if you wish, or leave them raw, and slice and lightly butter two or three slices of bread. When the bacon is ready, arrange it on your chosen bread, cover with the middle slice of bread (if used), cover with tomato slices and top with lettuce, adding sauce or ketchup to taste.

Brie and Cranberry
Put slices of Brie onto the bread and top with cranberry sauce.

Cheese
Slice or grate the cheese.

Cheese Slices
Quick and easy. Use straight from the packet. Spread pickle or chutney on top of the cheese if liked.

Cheese and Onion
Peel and thinly slice an onion, then lay it thinly on top of the sliced cheese.

Cheese and Pickle or Chutney
As above, and mix with a little pickle or chutney.

Cheese and Tomato
Slice a tomato layer on top of the cheese.

Cream Cheese and Cucumber
Spread the bread with cream cheese and top with cucumber slices.

Cold Meat
Sliced, cooked meat, from the supermarket or delicatessen: ham, tongue, turkey roll, chicken roll, salami, garlic sausage, etc. Buy according to your taste and pocket. Buy fresh as you need it; do not store too long in the fridge.

Cold Meat from the Joint
Beef and Mustard or Horseradish Sauce
Slice the beef thinly, and spread with the mustard or horseradish.

Cold Lamb and Mint Sauce
Slice the meat, cut off any excess fat. Add the mint sauce.

Cold Pork and Apple Sauce and Stuffing
Slice the pork, spread with any leftover apple sauce and stuffing.

Cold Chicken
Use up the fiddly bits from a roast chicken or buy chicken roll slices. Spread with cranberry jelly and stuffing. Do not store for too long in the fridge; buy just a little at a time.

Coronation Chicken
Buy a small carton from the deli counter at the supermarket, and spread on buttered brown or white bread.

Egg
Cook for 10 minutes in boiling water. Shell, wash and mash with a fork. Mix it either with a little mayonnaise or tomato chutney. One egg will fill two rounds of cut bread sandwiches.

Marmite
Very good for you, especially with a chunk of cheese or topped with sliced cheese.

Nutella and Banana
Spread the bread with Nutella and top with sliced banana – eat before the banana goes brown.

Peanut Butter
No need to butter the bread first. Top with seedless jam (jelly) if liked.

Salad
Washed lettuce, sliced tomato, sliced cucumber, layered together.

Salmon
Open a can, drain off any excess juice, and tip the salmon into a bowl. Discard the bones and skin, and mash with a little vinegar

and pepper. Spread on the buttered bread, top with cucumber slices or lettuce if liked.

Tuna Fish
Open a can, drain off the oil or water. Tip the tuna fish into a bowl and mash with vinegar and pepper, or mayonnaise. Spread on the buttered bread, top with lettuce or cucumber slices.

Liver Pâté
Choose from the numerous smooth or rough pâtés in the supermarket. Brown or granary bread is particularly good with pâté.

Eat with your Packed Lunch

Cottage Cheese (plain or flavoured)
Eat from the carton with a fresh buttered roll, or an apple if you're slimming. Don't forget to take a spoon.

Yogurt
Eat from the carton – remember to take a spoon.

Hardboiled Egg
Hard boil an egg. Shell and wash it. Pop it into a polythene bag and eat with a fresh buttered roll.

Scotch Egg
Buy fresh from the supermarket.

Crudités
Fresh and crunchy to go with your sandwich. Choose a good variety of raw vegetables cut into finger-sized sticks or bite-sized chunks (or buy a packet of ready-to-eat crudités from the supermarket) and take a little sealed pot of your favourite dip to eat with them. See the recipe on page 67.

TOASTED SANDWICHES

A freshly toasted sandwich, served with some green salad, coleslaw and potato salad, makes a super lunch or supper. It is easier to make a successful toasted sandwich if you have a Sandwich Toaster or a 'Toasta Bag' (a special reusable 'envelope' that can go in an ordinary toaster, available in hardware stores or departments and by mail order), but you can cook your sandwich under a hot grill or fry in the frying pan.

Sandwich Toaster
Prepare the sandwich and cook according to the toaster instruction book.

Toasta Bag
Prepare the sandwich and cook according to the instructions. Don't cut the bread too thick to fit in the toaster!

Grilling
Make the sandwich and cook under a hot grill, turning the sandwich over to cook both sides.

Frying
Prepare the sandwich, heat a *little* oil in the frying pan and fry the sandwich *gently* on both sides until golden brown.

FRIED CHEESE SANDWICHES

Serves 1

A very quick and tasty snack.

Takes 10 minutes

2–4 slices of bread
12 g/$^1/_2$ oz butter
2–4 thin cheese slices (a nice strong Cheddar or
  Mozzarella is good, or use pre-packed cheese slices
  if you prefer)
1 tbsp cooking oil and a large knob of butter (for frying)

Extra fillings (optional)
1 thinly sliced tomato
1 tsp pickle or chutney
1–2 rashers of crisply fried bacon – fry this ready
  before you start the sandwiches

Lightly butter the slices of bread. Make them into sandwiches
with one or two slices of cheese in each sandwich, adding any of
the optional extras you like.

Heat the oil and knob of butter in a frying pan over a moderate
heat. Put the sandwiches into the hot fat, and fry for a few minutes on each side, until the bread is golden and crispy, and the
cheese is beginning to melt.

Remove from the pan, drain on a piece of kitchen paper if they
seem a bit greasy. Eat at once while hot.

BEANS (OR SPAGHETTI) ON TOAST

Serves 1

If you've never cooked these before, here is the method.

25 g/1 oz cheese (optional)
1 small (225 g/8 oz) tin beans, spaghetti, spaghetti hoops, etc
2–3 slices of bread
Butter

Grate the cheese, or chop it finely (if used).

Put the beans or spaghetti into a small saucepan, and heat slowly over a moderate heat, stirring occasionally (or heat in a bowl in the microwave). Toast the bread and spread one side of it with butter. When the beans are beginning to bubble, stir gently until they are thoroughly heated.

Put the toast onto a warm plate, and pour the beans on top of the buttered side. (Some people prefer the toast left at the side of the plate.) Sprinkle the cheese on top. Eat at once.

GARLIC MUSHROOMS

Serves 1

Delicious, but don't breathe over other people after eating these!
Serve with fried bacon to make it more substantial.

Takes 10 minutes

75–100 g/3–4 oz mushrooms
1 clove of fresh garlic (or garlic powder or garlic paste)
1–2 rashers of bacon (optional)
25 g/1 oz butter with 1 tsp cooking oil
2 thick slices of bread

Wash the mushrooms. Peel, chop and crush the fresh garlic, if
used. Fry the bacon and keep hot. Melt the butter and oil in a
saucepan over a moderate heat. Add the garlic (fresh, powder or
paste) and mushrooms

Stir well, and fry gently for 3–5 minutes, stirring and spooning the
garlic-flavoured butter over the mushrooms. While the mushrooms are cooking, toast the bread lightly, cut in half and put onto
a hot plate. Spoon the mushrooms onto the toast and pour the
remaining garlic butter over the top. Top with bacon, if used. Eat
at once.

PIZZA AND PIZZA TOPPINGS

There are so many makes, shapes and sizes of pizza available now, both fresh and frozen, that it hardly seems worth the effort of making your own. However, these commercial ones are usually improved by adding your own extras during the cooking, either when under the grill or in the oven, according to the instructions on the packet.

Use the cheaper, plainer pizzas as a base, and add some extra from the fridge for the last 5–10 minutes of cooking time by strewing them on top of the pizza:

Cheese
Use Cheddar or a variety of different cheeses – Mozzarella, blue cheeses, Brie, halloumi or feta – grated, crumbled or thinly sliced.

Ham
Chop and sprinkle over the pizza.

Salami, Garlic Sausage
Chop or fold slices and arrange on top of the pizza.

Mushrooms
Wash and slice thinly, spread over the pizza.

Tomatoes
Slice thinly, spread over the pizza.

Olives
A few spread on top add colour and flavour.

Anchovies or Sardines
Arrange criss-cross on top of all the other toppings.

Roast Vegetables
Use leftover mixed roast vegetables (see page 110) or cook a few extra on purpose! Spread the cooked vegetables over a tomato base pizza, and top with a little grated cheese if liked.

BASIC GREEN SALAD

Serves 1

Takes 5 minutes

3–4 washed lettuce leaves
$1/_2$ small onion
1 tbsp vinaigrette (see page 72)

Leave the lettuce leaves whole if small, or shred as finely as you like. Peel and slice the onion. Put the lettuce and onion into a salad bowl, add the vinaigrette and lightly turn the lettuce over in the dressing until well mixed.

Other salad vegetables can be added:

Beetroot – bought ready cooked and sliced or
    diced to serve
Celery – washed, scraped if necessary, cut
    into 2.5 cm/1 inch lengths
Cucumber – washed, cut into rings or chunks
Pepper – washed, cored, cut into rings
Radishes – with tops cut off, roots removed, and washed
Spring onion – washed, cut off roots and yellow leaves,
    cut into rings or leave whole
Tomatoes – washed, sliced or cut into quarters
Watercress, mustard and cress – washed, sprinkled on
    top of the other vegetables

WINTER SALAD

Serves 1

Trim, shred and wash a quarter of a white or green cabbage. Drain well and dry in a salad shaker (if you have one) or put into a clean tea-towel and shake or pat dry. Put the cabbage in a dish with any other salad vegetables such as raw carrot batons, tomato quarters, cucumber, celery, peppers and sliced onions or chopped salad onions.

It can either by served on its own, or with a dressing made from the following ingredients mixed together thoroughly: 4 tsp salad oil, 2 tsp vinegar, pinch of salt, pepper and sugar.

GARLIC BREAD

Hot garlic bread is lovely with lots of snacks and salads. There are lots of packs available – fresh, frozen, low fat – so choose the kind that you like best. Just follow the instructions on the packet and you'll have hot, garlicky bread in a few minutes. If you don't like garlic (or don't want to breathe garlic for the rest of the day) try Herb Bread instead.

GREEK SALAD

Serves 1

Often served as a side dish with meat or fish, but a good large salad with plenty of feta cheese makes a nice summer lunch, served with warm bread rolls or pitta bread.

Takes 10 minutes

4 crisp lettuce leaves – Cos, Little Gem or mixed salad leaves
$1/_2$ small onion
A few radishes
5 cm/2 inch chunk of cucumber
2 tomatoes
Black and/or green olives
50 g/2 oz Greek feta cheese – if you can't get feta, use
   a hard crumbly white cheese (Lancashire is delicious)
1–2 tbsp salad dressing (traditionally vinaigrette)

Wash and dry the lettuce leaves, arrange in pieces on a serving plate. Peel and slice the onion into thin rings and scatter over the lettuce. Wash the radishes, slice and add to the salad. Wash the cucumber, cut into dice, wash and cut the tomatoes into slices or chunks, and arrange both on the salad mixture, sprinkling the olives over the top. Cut the cheese into bite-sized dice and pile in the centre of the dish. When you are ready to eat, pour the salad dressing over the salad and serve.

CREAMY AVOCADO TOAST

Serves 1

Use a soft, ripe avocado that will mash into a creamy paste.

Takes 5 minutes

1 ripe avocado
2 tsp mayonnaise
2 thick slices of bread for toast – granary is really nice
Butter or spread for toast

Cut the avocado in half lengthways and remove the stone. Spoon the avocado into a basin, mash to a soft cream with a fork and stir in the mayo. Toast the bread, spread with butter or spread and pile the avocado on top. Eat while the toast is hot, with a good green salad garnish.

SAVOURY AVOCADO SNACK

Serves 1

If you're vegetarian, omit the ham. This recipe also makes a good baguette filling, to be eaten cold.

Takes 15 minutes

1 small avocado pear
25–50 g/1–2 oz cheese – Cheddar, blue cheese or Brie
    according to taste
Length of French bread – according to appetite
Butter or spread
2 slices cooked ham (optional)
1 tbsp broken walnuts (optional)

Peel the avocado and slice lengthways, removing the stone. Slice the chosen cheese.

Split the French bread in half, spread with butter or spread. Arrange layers of avocado, then ham or chopped walnuts on the bread, and top with grated or sliced cheese. Cook under a hot grill for a few minutes until the cheese is melted. Eat at once.

CRUDITÉS

Good as a starter or light snack or to eat with your packed lunch. Use a good variety of raw vegetables cut into finger-sized sticks or bite-sized chunks. Choose your favourite vegetables and enjoy them with your favourite dips.

Takes 10–15 minutes

Vegetables

1 carrot – washed, peeled and cut into fingers

1 x 5 cm/2 inch piece cucumber – washed and cut into fingers or chunks

1–2 sticks celery – washed and cut into thin lengths

$1/_2$ small red or yellow pepper – washed, seeds removed and sliced

Few raw cauliflower florets – washed and broken into tiny florets

A few big radishes – roots cut off, washed, halved or served whole

3 or 4 mushrooms – washed and sliced or left whole if tiny

Few tiny spring onions – washed and trimmed

5 or 6 sugar snap peas – washed, topped and tailed, and served whole

DIPS

You can buy ready prepared dips from the supermarket or make your own using 2–3 tbsp mayonnaise for each dip.

Garlic
Beat in $1/4$ tsp garlic paste or a crushed clove of garlic.

Curry
Beat in $1/4$ tsp curry powder or paste, cayenne pepper or a very few drops of hot pepper sauce.

Marie Rose
Beat in $1/2$ tsp tomato purée or ketchup.

Blue Cheese
Mash 25 g/1 oz blue cheese to a paste and mix it into the mayonnaise.

Spoon the dips into individual pots. Serve the crudités on a plate with the pot of dip surrounded by little piles of vegetables, garnished with mixed salad leaves.

Hummus, tsatsiki and taramasalata can be served in the same way.

For a party, serve large dishes of dips, with plenty of crudités, crisps and pieces of warm pitta bread.

Packed lunch – take a selection of prepared crudités in a sandwich box or polythene bag, with a carton of your favourite dip to eat with your sandwiches.

RICE SALAD

This is nicest if you make a larger quantity, either to serve two people or to eat half and keep the rest in the fridge to eat tomorrow, as you can then put a good variety of salad veg and fruit into the rice. Use white or brown rice according to taste.

Takes 30–40 minutes

100 g/4 oz/1 full cup long grain rice – white or brown
1 tsp cooking oil or knob of butter
1–2 eggs
1–2 tbsp salad dressing – vinaigrette or your favourite
   flavour

Choose a good mixture of salad vegetables to add to the rice
2–3 tbsp drained canned sweetcorn kernels
1 large tomato – washed, sliced and chopped
2 cm/1 inch cucumber – washed and chopped
Large slice of red pepper – washed and chopped
Large slice of green pepper – washed and chopped
1 tbsp sultanas – washed and dried
1 tbsp chopped walnuts
1 tbsp pine kernels
1 or 2 spring onions – trimmed, washed and finely
   snipped
2–3 tbsp vinaigrette dressing (see page 72) or salad
   dressing of your choice
Few sprigs parsley – washed and finely snipped

Prepare and cook the chosen rice as described on page 116.

Hard boil the eggs, remove the shells and cut into quarters (see page 23).

Assemble and prepare the chosen vegetables, nuts and seeds.

When the rice is cooked, drain well, tip into a serving bowl and mix the chosen salad dressing into the hot rice.

Stir the prepared chosen vegetables carefully into the rice, saving some of the snipped spring onions and parsley for later.

Arrange the pieces of egg on top.

Sprinkle the rest of the snipped spring onions and parsley on top when ready to serve.

TABBOULEH

Serves 1–2 according to appetite

This salad is good eaten with grilled meat or fish, or as an accompaniment with a barbecue. Any leftover salad will keep overnight in the fridge, and will make a light lunch with cold meat and/or hardboiled eggs and fresh bread rolls.

Takes 10 minutes + 1 hour for soaking

100 g/4 oz/4 very heaped tbsp bulgar or cracked wheat
3–4 spring onions
Small bunch fresh chives
Small bunch fresh parsley and/or coriander
Small bunch fresh mint
2–3 tbsp olive oil or vegetable oil
2 tbsp lemon juice or juice of $^1/_2$ lemon
Salt and pepper

Put the bulgar or cracked wheat in a large bowl or pan, add cold water to cover the wheat and half fill the bowl. Leave to soak for an hour.

Strain the wheat well in a sieve, and squeeze as dry as possible. Dry the bowl and tip the wheat back into it.

Trim (retaining as much of the green part as looks appetizing), wash and dry the spring onions. Finely chop or scissor-snip the onions and stir into the wheat.

Wash, dry and finely chop the chives, parsley and coriander into the wheat.

Strip the leaves of mint stalks, wash, dry and chop or snip them finely into the wheat mixture. Mix the wheat and herbs together well, add the chosen oil and season to taste with the lemon juice, salt and pepper.

If you have fresh herbs available in the garden or in pots, experiment by adding a few washed, finely snipped sprigs of thyme, rosemary, lemon balm, tarragon, etc, to the other herbs, according to taste and availability.

VINAIGRETTE OR FRENCH DRESSING

Serves 1

A handy salad dressing to make yourself and keep in the fridge (in a small, screw-top jar). It will keep for weeks in a cold place, and is the most widely used dressing for all kinds of salads. It's very quick to make and you can add your favourite flavourings to the basic recipe when you mix the ingredients – use flavoured vinegar or plain lemon juice, add a pinch of garlic or herbs or use honey instead of sugar. Olive and walnut oils give the best flavour but are more expensive than most other vegetable oils. Wine vinegar has a less harsh flavour than malt vinegar, and a shake of Balsamic vinegar makes it very smooth, but they can all make a delicious dressing.

For one serving
2 tsp olive or other vegetable oil
1 tsp vinegar and/or lemon juice
Pinch of salt, black pepper, mustard and sugar
Few drops Balsamic vinegar

Put all the ingredients in a basin or cup and stir with a teaspoon until well mixed. Pour over salad, turning gently to coat all the ingredients with the dressing.

To make a jarful

Use proportions of 2 lots of oil to 1 lot of vinegar

Pour into a small, screwtop jar:
70 ml/2 fl oz/$^1/_2$ cup olive oil or other vegetable oil
35 ml/1 fl oz/$^1/_4$ cup vinegar and/or lemon juice
$^1/_4$ tsp salt
$^1/_4$ tsp black pepper
$^1/_4$ tsp mustard
$^1/_2$–1 tsp white sugar – according to taste
$^1/_2$–1 tsp Balsamic vinegar

Screw the lid firmly on the jar. Shake well for 1–2 minutes until thoroughly mixed. Store in the fridge and shake again before use. If the dressing solidifies, stand the jar in hot (not boiling) water for a few minutes before use.

4
VEGETABLES AND VEGETABLE DISHES

This section explains how to prepare and cook fresh vegetables (listed in alphabetical order), bought from the market, greengrocer or supermarket, to be eaten as part of a meal, followed by recipes which are substantial enough to be used as a lunch or supper dish by themselves.

When cooking vegetables in water, remember that a lot of the goodness and flavour soaks from the vegetables into the cooking water, so do not use too much water or overcook them and, when possible, use the cooking water for making gravy or sauce. There is no need to add salt to the cooking water, as apparently we all eat too much salt these days!

Try to buy only the amount of vegetables you will need, as leftover veg usually get lost in the cupboard or fridge until thrown out and wasted. It's easy to get carried away by the bargains on the market stall or the 'buy one and get one half price' at the supermarket – an expensive bargain if you waste half of it! Vegetable prices may vary according to the season, so look out for the best buys, and remember that the nice little packets of pre-packed vegetables are delicious and ready to cook, but are usually quite expensive.

Frozen vegetables are convenient, if you have a freezer to keep them in, as they are usually sold in rather large packs. Chips and other potato products are useful, and peas, broad beans, etc, that are only available fresh for a very short season are good too, but make sure there is enough space in the freezer before you buy these big packets that must be kept frozen.

GLOBE ARTICHOKES

These are the green, leafy type of artichoke. They look large, but as you only eat the bottom tip of each leaf, you do need *a whole artichoke for each person*. As they are expensive, cook them mainly for special occasions.

Cut off the stem of the artichoke to make the base level, snip off the points of the leaves, and wash the artichoke well in cold water. Put in a large saucepan, cover with boiling water and boil for 30–40 minutes, until a leaf will pull off easily.

Drain the water from the pan and then turn the artichoke upside down in the pan for a few moments to drain any remaining water. Serve with plenty of butter.

JERUSALEM ARTICHOKES

These artichokes look like knobbly potatoes. Cook them immediately they are peeled, as they go brown very quickly even in cold water. A little lemon juice in the cooking water helps to keep them white.

225 g/8 oz serves 1–2 portions.

BOILED
Peel the artichokes and cut them into evenly-sized lumps about the size of small potatoes. Boil them in a pan of water for 20–30 minutes until tender. Drain and serve with a dab of butter.

FRIED
Peel the artichokes and cut them into thick slices or chunks. Put 1 tsp cooking oil and 12 g/$^1/_2$ oz butter into a frying pan, add the artichoke pieces and cook gently, turning frequently, for 15–20 minutes, until soft. Tip the artichokes onto a warm plate, pouring the buttery sauce over them.

ASPARAGUS

A real treat, now available all year round, although at its best in the summer when English asparagus is in season. In some parts of the country you can buy it fresh from the asparagus farm or even 'pick your own'.

Asparagus is usually sold in bundles, enough for 2–3 servings, if eaten as a starter with mayonnaise.

Asparagus needs very little cooking, and can be gently simmered in water on top of the stove, steamed, or cooked in the microwave. It is nice in a green salad or added raw to a pan of roast vegetables for the last few minutes at the end of their cooking time, and can also be cooked on the barbecue. The heads are very delicate so take care not to break them off during preparation.

SIMMERING
Cut off the end of each shoot and rinse well. Lay the asparagus flat in a very clean, grease-free frying pan and just cover with hot water. Bring to the boil, turn down the heat immediately to a light simmer, and cook for 3–4 minutes, or less if you like it crunchy. Turn off the heat and carefully remove the asparagus from the pan using a fish slice or slotted spoon. Arrange on a plate, garnish with lettuce and cucumber and serve with mayonnaise and brown bread and butter.

STEAMING
Lay the asparagus flat in a steamer, cover with a lid and cook over a pan of boiling water for 6–8 minutes. Serve as above.

Microwaving

Lay the asparagus flat in a microwaveable dish, adding 2–3 tbsp water, and cover with plastic film. Cook on high for 1–2 minutes or as advised in your microwave cookbook. Serve as above.

Barbecuing

This only takes a few minutes. It's best cooked on a narrow grid or a baking tray. Brush with melted butter and turn frequently until cooked.

AUBERGINES

These lovely, shiny, purple-skinned vegetables are left unpeeled as the skins give extra taste and texture.

They can be fried on their own, added to mixed roast vegetables (page 110) or made into a delicious supper dish (page 107).

Fry 1 small aubergine per person.

Wash and dry the aubergine, cut into 1 cm/$^1/_2$ inch slices, and brush both sides with cooking oil. Heat a little more oil in a frying pan and fry the slices gently until browned and soft. Be careful not to use much oil, as aubergines soak up oil like sponges!

Aubergine slices can be fried with sauté potatoes (page 97).

AVOCADO PEARS

Delicious, nutritious and very good for you, especially if you are a vegetarian. Choose pears that yield slightly when pressed gently. Unripe pears feel very hard, although they should ripen eventually if left in a warm place.

Slice the avocado in half lengthways, cutting through to the stone. Then separate the two halves by twisting gently. Remove the stone with the tip of the knife, trying not to damage the flesh, which should be soft and buttery in texture.

Cut avocados discolour very quickly, so prepare them just before serving. Serve avocados plain with a squeeze of lemon juice, with a vinaigrette dressing or with any one of the numerous fillings suggested overleaf spooned into the cavity from where the stone was removed. Brown bread and butter is the traditional accompaniment, with a garnish of lettuce, tomato and cucumber.

QUICK TIP *To stop avocados discolouring when cut, half fill a large saucepan with gently boiling water. Carefully immerse the avocado in the water (use a large spoon) and turn it over in the hot water for 2–3 seconds to make sure it is completely covered by the water. Remove at once and cool in cold water before using. This will prevent avocados discolouring for several hours – **it really does work!***

Some Filling Ideas

Vinaigrette
Mix well 2 tsp oil, 1 tsp vinegar, salt, pepper and a pinch of sugar.

Mayonnaise
1 tbsp mayonnaise.

Cottage Cheese
Mix well together 2 tbsp cottage cheese (plain or with chives, pineapple, etc) and 1 tsp mayonnaise.

Prawn or Shrimp
Mix gently together 1–2 tbsp shelled prawns or shrimps (fresh, frozen or canned), 1 tbsp mayonnaise and/or cottage cheese. A sauce can also be made with a mixture of 1 tbsp salad cream and a dish of tomato ketchup.

Egg
Shell and chop one hard-boiled egg. Mix gently with 2 tbsp mayonnaise and/or cottage cheese.

Yogurt
2 tbsp yogurt on its own, or mixed with a chopped tomato and a few slices chopped cucumber.

BROAD BEANS

Fresh broad beans are most usually available in the summer, but you need a lot of pods to produce enough beans for a meal.

Allow 225 g/8 oz pods per person.

Remove the beans from the pods. Cook in gently boiling water for 5–6 minutes, until tender. Drain and serve with a knob of butter, or parsley sauce (see page 228).

Frozen Broad Beans

The easiest way to eat broad beans!

Allow 100 g/4 oz per serving.

Cook as instructed on the packet, and serve as above.

FRENCH BEANS

Buy a small pack as there is very little waste, but extra beans will keep fresh for a few days in the fridge.

Top and tail the beans with a vegetable knife or a pair of scissors. Wash the beans and cut the longer beans in half (about 10 cm/4 inches). Put them into a pan of boiling water and cook for 2–5 minutes, until just tender. Drain well and serve with a knob of butter. Cooked beans are also delicious served cold as part of a salad.

RUNNER BEANS

Fresh beans from abroad are available all year round, but nothing beats lovely fresh beans from the garden in the summer.

Choose crisp green beans – limp, pallid ones are not very fresh.

Allow 100 g/4 oz beans per person.

Top and tail the beans, cut down each side to remove any stringy bits, and slice evenly into pieces into 2 cm/1 inch long. Rinse in cold water, then cook in boiling water for 5–10 minutes until just tender, not too soft. Drain well and serve hot.

BEAN SPROUTS

These can be cooked on their own, but are better when cooked with a mixture of stir-fried vegetables – see page 134.

Bean sprouts are delicious eaten raw or in a salad – rinse them well, soak in a pan of cold water for a few minutes. Drain, pat dry on kitchen paper and add to a green or mixed salad.

BROCCOLI

Green and purple sprouting broccoli are both cooked in the same way.

Allow 3–4 pieces per serving.

Cut off the stalk, divide the broccoli into equal sized florets. Wash in cold water. Put in a pan, cover with hot water and boil gently for 4–6 minutes until tender but still crisp. Drain well and serve.

BRUSSELS SPROUTS

Try to buy firm, green sprouts of approximately the same size. Yellow outside leaves are a sign of old age.

Allow 100–150 g/4–6 oz per serving.

Cut off the stalk ends and trim off the outer leaves if necessary. Wash well. Cook in boiling water for 5–10 minutes until tender. Drain well.

FROZEN SPROUTS

Allow 75–100 g/3–4 oz per serving.

Cook in boiling water as directed on the packet.

WHITE OR GREEN CABBAGE

A much maligned vegetable, evoking memories of school days. If cooked properly, cabbage is really delicious and much cheaper than a lot of other vegetables. Cabbage goes a very long way, so either buy a *small cabbage* and use it for several meals (cooked, or raw in a winter salad) or *just buy half or a quarter of a cabbage.*

Trim off the outer leaves and the stalk. Cut into quarters and shred, not too finely, removing the central core and cutting that into small pieces. Wash the cabbage. Boil it in a little water for 2–5 minutes. Do not overcook. Drain well, serve with a knob of butter, or with a cheese sauce.

To make cabbage cheese instead of cauliflower cheese, substitute the cabbage for the cauliflower on page 48.

CRUNCHY FRIED CABBAGE

Trim, shred and wash the cabbage as above. Heat a little butter and 1–2 tsp vegetable oil in a pan, add the cabbage and fry gently for 3–4 minutes, adding $1/2$ tsp mixed dried herbs if liked. Serve hot.

CARROTS

New carrots can simply be scrubbed and cooked whole, like new potatoes. Older, larger carrots should be scraped or peeled, then cut in halves, quarters, slices, rings or dice, as preferred. The smaller the pieces, the quicker the carrots will cook.

Allow 100 g/4 oz per serving.

Scrub, peel and slice the carrots as necessary. Boil them in water for 5–20 minutes, according to their size, until just tender. Serve with a knob of butter.

BUTTERED CARROTS

Prepare the carrots as above: leaving tender, young carrots whole or slicing old carrots into rings. Put the carrots in a saucepan, with $^1/_2$ a cup of water, 12 g/$^1/_2$ oz butter, and 1 tsp sugar. Bring to the boil, then reduce the heat and simmer for about 20 minutes, until the carrots are tender. Take the lid off the saucepan, turn up the heat for a few minutes, and let the liquid bubble away until only a little sauce is left. Put the carrots onto a plate, and pour the sauce over them.

CAULIFLOWER

Most cauliflowers are too large for one person, but they can be cut in half and the remainder kept in the fridge for use in the next few days. Try not to bruise the florets when cutting them, as they will discolour easily. Very small caulis and packets of cauliflower florets are sold in some supermarkets.

Allow 3–4 florets per serving.

Trim off tough stems and outer leaves. The cauli can either be left whole or divided into florets. Wash thoroughly. Cook in boiling water for 5–15 minutes, according to size, until just tender. Drain well. Serve hot with a knob of butter, a spoonful of soured cream, or white sauce (see page 228). For cauliflower cheese, see page 48.

FROZEN CAULIFLOWER

Allow 100–150 g/4–5 oz per serving.

Cook as directed on the packet and serve as above.

CELERIAC

The root of a variety of celery, celeriac is one of the more unusual vegetables now available in good greengrocers and larger supermarkets.

Allow 100–225 g/4–8 oz per person.

Peel fairly thickly and cut into evenly-sized chunks. Put into a saucepan with boiling water, and cook for 30–40 minutes until soft. Drain well. Serve with butter or mash with a potato masher, fork or whisk, with a little butter and top of the milk. Season with salt and pepper.

CELERY

Most popular eaten raw, with cheese or chopped up in a salad. It can be cooked and served as a hot vegetable; the tougher outer stems can be used for cooking, leaving the tender inner stems to be eaten raw.

Allow 3–4 stalks of celery per serving.

Trim the celery stalk. Divide it into separate stems. Wash each stem well and scrape off any stringy bits with a knife. The celery is now ready to eat raw. To cook, chop the celery into 2.5 cm/1 inch lengths. Put it into a saucepan, with boiling water, and cook for 10 minutes until just tender. Drain well, serve with a knob of butter, or put into a greased ovenproof dish, top with 25–50 g/1–2 oz grated cheese, and brown under a hot grill.

CHICORY

This can be used raw in salads, or cooked carefully in water and butter, and served hot.

Allow 175–225 g/6–8 oz/one head per serving.

Remove any damaged outer leaves and trim the stalk. With a pointed vegetable knife, cut a cone-shaped core out of the base, to ensure even cooking and reduce bitterness. Wash in cold water. Put the chicory into a saucepan with a knob of butter and 2–4 tbsp water. Cook gently for about 20 minutes, until just tender, making sure that all the liquid does not disappear. Serve with melted butter.

CHINESE LEAVES OR PAK CHOI

These can be used raw in salads. Keep the Chinese leaves in a polythene bag in the fridge to keep them crisp until you want to use them.

Allow $1/_4$– $1/_2$ small cabbage per serving.

Trim off any spoiled leaves and stalks. Shred finely. Wash and drain well (in a salad shaker or a clean tea-towel). Use in salad with any other salad vegetables (cucumber, tomato, cress, spring onions, radish, etc) and a vinaigrette dressing (2 tbsp oil, 1 tsp vinegar, pinch of salt, pepper and sugar, all mixed well together), or your favourite salad dressing.

COURGETTES

These are baby marrows. They are quick and easy to prepare, and are quite economical as there is almost no waste with them.

Allow 1 or 2 courgettes per serving, according to size.

Courgettes are nicest fried, as they go very watery if boiled.

FRIED

Top and tail the courgettes. Wash, dry and slice them into 1 cm/$\frac{1}{2}$ inch rings. Melt a little cooking oil and butter in a frying pan, add courgettes and fry gently for a few minutes until soft and lightly browned. Season with salt, pepper, fresh snipped parsley or a pinch of dried herbs. Serve hot.

For a change, fry 1 or 2 sliced tomatoes with the courgettes – this is very good with fish or as an accompaniment to a main meal.

LEEKS

These must be carefully prepared or they will taste gritty.

Allow 1 or 2 leeks per serving according to size and appetite.

Cut off the roots and peel off all the tough, dirty outside leaves, until you reach the soft green leaves and the clean white leek, with no dirt left on the leeks. Wipe the outside thoroughly with damp kitchen paper, and then cut the leeks into thin rings.

Heat a little oil and butter in a pan and sauté the cut leeks over a gentle heat for 5–10 minutes until soft. Stir in a pinch of dried mixed herbs, season to taste with salt and pepper, and snip some fresh parsley or coriander over the leeks, if available, and serve.

LETTUCE

There are so many different kinds of lettuce readily available, all nice, and everyone has their favourite. Choose a lettuce that looks crisp and firm, with a solid heart – if it looks limp and flabby, it is old and stale. Lettuce will only keep fresh for a few days, even in a polythene bag or box in the fridge, so buy a *small lettuce* unless you're going to eat a lot of salad!

Cut off the stalk and discard any dirty or battered leaves. Pull the leaves off the stem, wash them in cold water and dry them thoroughly in a salad shaker or pat dry in a clean tea-towel. Tear or slice the leaves and serve as a basic green salad, or a side salad with hot dishes (either tossed in dressing or with the dressing served separately), or use as a garnish for all kinds of dishes.

The ready prepared bags of mixed salad leaves are very useful when catering for one person, as they provide variety without having to buy a mountain of lettuce!

MARROW

Very cheap when in season during the autumn – it can be eaten peeled, sliced into chunks and simmered in boiling water for 5 minutes, drained well and served as a vegetable with meat or fish, but it is very watery and rather tasteless. It is far nicer filled with a tasty stuffing and baked in the oven (see page 114).

MUSHROOMS

Buy in small amounts so that they can be eaten fresh. Fresh mushrooms look plump and firm, older ones look dried up and brownish. Store mushrooms in the fridge in a *paper* bag or the carton in which they were bought. Mushrooms can be fried or grilled with bacon, sausages, eggs, steak, etc. Add them to casseroles or stews or make a tasty snack by cooking them in butter and garlic and serving on toast (see page 60).

Allow 2–4 mushrooms each – they shrink as they cook.

FRIED
Rinse mushrooms in cold water and dry well with kitchen paper. Leave whole or slice large ones. Fry them gently in a little butter and oil until soft. They can be put in the frying pan with bacon or sausages, or cooked separately in a smaller saucepan.

GRILLED
Rinse as above, then put a small knob of butter in each mushroom and grill them for a few minutes in the base of the grill pan! If you are grilling them with meat or sausages, put the mushrooms under the grill rack – the juice from the meat and mushrooms together makes a tasty sauce.

BAKED

Allow 1–3 large flat mushrooms per person.

Rinse and dry the mushrooms and put into a well greased ovenproof dish or tin. Top with a large knob of butter and bake for 10–20 minutes in a hot oven (200°C/400°F/Fan 180°C/Gas Mark 6). If liked, top each mushroom with a slice of cheese (Cheddar, Blue or Brie) for the last 5 minutes of cooking.

ONIONS

The best way to peel onions without crying is to cut off the tops and tails and then peel the skins with a sharp vegetable knife, working as quickly as possible.

To chop or slice onions evenly, slice the peeled onion downwards, vertically, into even sliced rings, then hold the rings together, turn them sideways and slice the rings through again to chop them finely.

ROAST ONION

Allow 1 medium or large onion per person.

Spanish onions are good for roasting. Top, tail and peel the onion. Heat a little oil or fat in a roasting tin (200°C/400°F/Fan 180°C/Gas Mark 6). When hot (3–5 minutes), place the onion carefully in the hot fat – it will spit, beware! Roast for 45 minutes to 1 hour. Onions are delicious roasted with a joint of meat and roast potatoes.

BAKED ONION

Allow 1 large onion per person.

Spanish onions are the best. Rinse the onion, top and tail it, but do not peel it. Put it in a tin or baking dish, and bake for 45 minutes to 1 hour (200°C/400°F/Fan 180°C/Gas Mark 6). Slit and serve with butter.

FRIED ONION

Allow 1 onion per person.

Top, tail and peel the onion and slice into rings. Fry them gently in a saucepan with a little oil and butter, for 5–10 minutes, until soft and golden, stirring occasionally. Delicious with liver and bacon.

PARSNIPS

These are very tasty and can be roasted on their own, with roast potatoes or as part of mixed roast vegetables.

Allow 1 parsnip per person if small, or a large parsnip will cut into 5 or 6 pieces.

Parsnips are cooked in the same way as roast potatoes (see page 96), but don't cut them into too many small pieces or they get too crispy. If you peel them before you are ready to cook them, keep them covered in a pan of cold water, as they go brown very quickly. (If this should happen, the parsnips will still be all right to cook; they will just look a bit speckled.)

PEAS

Most commonly sold frozen or tinned, but fresh garden peas are a real treat in the summer, so try some – it's fun shelling them.

Allow 250 g/8 oz peas in the pod per serving.

Shell the peas and remove any maggoty ones. Boil the peas gently in water, with a sprig of mint if possible for 5–10 minutes. Drain well, remove the mint and stir in a sprinkle of sugar. Serve topped with a small knob of butter.

TINNED PEAS
A small (225 g) tin should serve two helpings. Cook as directed on the tin and store any leftovers in a basin in the fridge.

MUSHY PEAS

These are sold in tins and are very good with fish. Cook as directed on the tin. Store leftovers in a basin in the fridge.

FROZEN PEAS

Only buy these if you have a freezer, unless you are cooking for several people and will use the whole packet.

Allow 75–100 g/3–4 oz per serving.

Add a handful of mangetout or sugar snap peas to frozen peas and cook them together to make frozen peas more special!

MANGETOUT AND SUGAR SNAP PEAS

A special treat, but they can be bought in small amounts and you eat the lot, including the pods.

Allow 50–75 g/2–4 oz per serving.

Top and tail the pods with scissors, wash the pods and leave them whole. Cook in a pan of gently boiling water for 2–3 minutes – they should still be slightly crunchy when cooked. Serve hot with a knob of butter if liked.

Both mangetout and sugar snap peas are lovely eaten raw with dips or in a salad.

GREEN, YELLOW, ORANGE AND RED PEPPERS

Use raw in a salad or with dips, add to roast vegetables (see page 110), or cook, filled with a tasty stuffing for a lunch or supper dish (see page 186).

Peppers can be bought singly. Choose crisp, firm looking ones and store them in the fridge to keep fresh.

Rinse the pepper in cold water, cut off the top, scoop out the core and the seeds. Cut into rings and use in salads or as a garnish.

POTATOES

Lots and lots of different varieties available from supermarkets and farm shops – try some of the different ones occasionally.

BOILED POTATOES

Try to select potatoes of the same size to cook together, or cut large potatoes into evenly-sized pieces, so that all the potatoes will be cooked at the same time. (Very big potatoes will go soggy on the outside before the inside is cooked if left whole.) Don't let the water boil too fast or the potatoes will tend to break up.

Allow 2–6 potato pieces per person.

Peel the potatoes as thinly as you can. Dig out any eyes or any black bits with as little waste as possible. Put them in a saucepan. Cover with hot water. Bring to the boil, then lower the heat and simmer for 15–20 minutes until they feel just soft when tested with a knife. Drain and serve hot.

MASHED POTATOES

This is the best way of serving boiled potatoes that have broken up during cooking. Prepare the boiled potatoes as described above. (If you are in a hurry, cut the potatoes into thick slices and cook for less time – about 10 minutes.) When they are cooked, drain the potatoes well. Mash them with a fork or masher until fluffy, then heap onto a serving dish.

CREAMED POTATOES

Prepare mashed potatoes as above. When they are really fluffy, beat in a knob of butter and a little top of the milk. Fork into a heap on a serving dish and top with a dab of butter.

POTATO CASTLES

Prepare creamed potatoes as above. Grease a flat baking tin or an ovenproof plate, and pile the potatoes onto it in two or three evenly-sized heaps. Fork them into castles, top with a bit of butter and either brown under the grill for a minute or two, or put them into a hot oven (200°C/400°F/Fan 180°C/Gas Mark 6) for 5–10 minutes, until crisp and golden brown.

CHEESY POTATOES

Prepare creamed potatoes as above, beating 25–50 g/1–2 oz grated cheese into the potatoes with the butter. Pile the potatoes into a greased ovenproof dish, fork down evenly and top with a little grated cheese. Brown under a hot grill for a minute or two, or put into a hot oven (200°C/400°F/Fan 180°C/Gas Mark 6) for 5–10 minutes, until golden.

ROAST POTATOES

Allow 3–6 (or more!) potato pieces each.

These can be cooked around the joint if you are cooking a roast dinner (*but not if you are serving a vegetarian*), or put in a separate roasting tin with a little hot oil, and cooked on their own.

Heat the oven at 200–220°C/400–425°F/Fan 180–200°C/Gas Mark 6–7.

Peel the potatoes and cut into even sized pieces (large or small as you prefer). Put them into a saucepan of hot water, bring to the boil and simmer for 3–5 minutes, according to size.

Meanwhile, put a roasting tin to heat in the oven, unless cooking potatoes around a joint of meat which may already be cooking.

Drain the potatoes and shake them in the pan *above* the heat to dry (*be very careful NOT to touch a ceramic hob while doing this or it will be scratched*).

Tip the potatoes into the roasting tin, add a little cooking oil and turn the potatoes over in this to coat all sides. Put the pan back into the hot oven and roast for 30–60 minutes, according to size, until crisp and golden brown.

Remove from the oven, put into a serving dish and keep them warm until ready to serve – *do not cover the dish, or the potatoes will not stay crispy.*

NEW POTATOES

Lovely and easy – no peeling!

Allow 3–6 new potatoes per person according to appetite.

Wash the potatoes in a bowl of water, digging out any eyes or black bits with a vegetable knife. Put them in a pan with a sprig of mint if possible, cover with boiling water and simmer for 15–20 minutes until tender. Drain, remove the mint and serve with butter.

SAUTÉ POTATOES

A way of using up leftover boiled or roast potatoes. Alternatively, potatoes can be boiled specially, and then sautéed when they have gone cold.

Allow approximately 3–4 cold cooked potato pieces, according to appetite.

Slice the potatoes thinly. Heat a little oil and butter in a frying pan. Add the potato slices and fry them gently for 5 minutes until crisp and golden, turning frequently with a fish slice or spatula.

ONION SAUTÉ POTATOES
Peel and thinly slice a small onion. Fry the onion in a frying pan with a little oil and butter until it is just soft, then add the cold, sliced potatoes and fry as above until crisp and delicious. Serve at once.

AUBERGINE SAUTÉ POTATOES
Prepare the aubergine slices (see page 78) and pat them dry. Prepare the sauté potatoes, and begin frying them in the pan in the hot oil and butter. Add a little more oil (not too much or the aubergines become greasy), add the aubergine and cook the vegetables together for a few minutes until crisp and golden. Serve at once.

JACKET SPUDS

These can be served as an accompaniment to meat or fish or made into a meal on their own, with any one of a number of fillings heaped on top of them.

Allow 1 medium–large potato per person.

Choose potatoes that don't have any mouldy-looking patches on the skin. Remember that very large potatoes will take longer to cook, so if you're hungry it's better to cook two medium-sized spuds. Wash and scrub the potato. Prick it several times with a fork. For quicker cooking, spear potatoes onto a metal skewer or potato baker.

TRADITIONAL WAY

Put the potato into the oven (200°C/400°F/Fan 180°C/Gas Mark 6) for 1–1½ hours according to size. The skin should be crisp and the inside soft and fluffy when ready. If you prefer softer skin, or don't want to risk the potato bursting all over the oven, wrap the spud loosely in a piece of cooking foil before putting it into the oven.

QUICKER WAY

Heat the oven at 200°C/400°F/Fan 180°C/Gas Mark 6. Put the potato into a saucepan, cover with hot water, bring to the boil and cook for 5–10 minutes according to size. Drain it carefully, lift the potato out with a cloth, and put into the hot oven for 30–60 minutes, according to size, until it feels soft.

If you are cooking a casserole in the oven at a lower temperature, put the potato in the oven with it, and allow extra cooking time.

JACKET SPUDS IN THE MICROWAVE

Wash and prick the potatoes, put in the microwave and cook on full power until soft (check your instruction book for timings). Heat the grill and grill the cooked spuds for a few minutes until the skins are crisp. If you have a combination microwave, follow the instruction book.

BAKED STUFFED POTATO

Useful to serve with cold meat or with steak, as it can be prepared in advance and heated up at the last minute.

Scrub and bake a largish jacket potato as described opposite. When the potato is soft, remove from the oven, and cut it carefully in half lengthways. Scoop the soft potato into a bowl, and mash with a fork, adding 12 g/$^1/_2$ oz butter and 12 g/$^1/_2$ oz grated cheese. Pile the filling back into the skin again and fork down evenly. Place on a baking tin or ovenproof plate, sprinkle a little grated cheese on top, and either brown under the hot grill for a few minutes, or put into a hot oven (200°C/400°F/Fan 180°C/Gas Mark 6) for 5–10 minutes until browned.

A FEW FILLINGS

Prepare and cook the jacket spuds. When soft, put them onto a plate, split open and top with your chosen filling and a knob of butter.

Cheese
25–50 g/1–2 oz grated cheese.

Cheese and Onion
1 small finely-sliced onion and 25–50 g/1–2 oz grated cheese.

Cheese and Pickle or Chutney
25–50 g/1–2 oz grated cheese and 1 tsp pickle or chutney.

Cottage Cheese
2–3 tbsp cottage cheese (plain or with chives, pineapple, etc).

Baked Beans
Heat a small tin of baked beans and pour over the potato.

Bolognese
Top with Bolognese sauce (see page 125). This is a good way of using up any extra sauce left over from Spaghetti Bolognese.

Bacon
Chop 1–2 rashers of bacon into pieces. Fry them for a few minutes, until crisp, then pour over the potato.

Egg
Top with 1–2 fried eggs, a scrambled egg or an omelette.

Curry
Top with any leftover curry sauce, heated gently in a saucepan until piping hot.

SCALLOPED POTATOES

Serves 2

Tasty and impressive-looking potatoes. Quick to prepare but they take an hour to cook, so they can be put in the oven and left while you are preparing the rest of the meal, or they can cook on a shelf above a casserole in the oven. (The potatoes need a higher temperature so put them on the top shelf and the casserole lower down.)

Allow 1–2 potatoes per person according to size and appetite.

Heat the oven at 200°C/400°F/Fan 180°C/Gas Mark 6.

Grease an ovenproof dish well. Peel the potatoes and slice them as thinly as possible. Put them in layers in the greased dish, sprinkling each layer with a little flour, salt and pepper. Almost cover them with $^1/_2$–1 cup of milk (or milk and water). Dot with a large knob of butter. Put the dish, uncovered, in the hot oven for about an hour, until the potatoes are soft and most of the liquid has been absorbed. The top should be crispy.

Packets of scalloped potatoes are available in supermarkets. They are more expensive than making your own, but are easy to prepare following the packet instructions.

CHIPS

Buy frozen oven chips and cook according to the instructions on the pack. There are so many different types: thick, thin, curly, wedges, croquettes – take your pick!

PUMPKIN

Generally associated with Halloween, Cinderella and American Thanksgiving Day! They are usually available fresh in the UK in October, in preparation for Halloween. The pumpkin flesh can be cooked like a swede (see opposite), then drained well, mashed and eaten as a vegetable or used to make Pumpkin Pie or Pumpkin Soup.

SPINACH

Allow 250 g/8 oz per person.

Preparing fresh spinach is rather tedious, so buy a bag of prepared spinach, all ready to cook, from the salad section of the supermarket, and cook following the instructions on the bag.

SQUASH

Different squashes appear in the shops all year round, and usually have suggestions for cooking them on display beside them. Butternut squash is very popular and can be baked or peeled, cut into chunks and added to soups and stews.

SWEDE ('NEEPS' IN SCOTLAND)

Known as 'poisonous' by one member of our family, but really it is a delicious winter vegetable.

Buy a very small swede for one person,
or a slightly larger one for 2 servings.

Peel thickly so that no brown or green skin remains. Cut into 1.25 cm/$^1/_2$ inch chunks. Cook in boiling water for 15–20 minutes until tender. Drain well (if you are making gravy at the same time, save the water for the gravy liquid), and mash with a fork or potato masher, adding a knob of butter and plenty of pepper.

If you wish, peel one or two carrots, cut them into rings and cook them with the swede, mashing the two vegetables together with butter as above, or just mix the two together without mashing.

SWEETCORN

The best fresh English sweetcorn cobs are in the shops from August to October, although imported sweetcorn is available throughout the year.

Cut off the stalk, remove the leaves and silky threads – this is a bit fiddly but try and pull all the threads off. Put the cobs into a pan of boiling *unsalted* water (salt makes the kernels tough), and simmer for 8–10 minutes, until the kernels are tender. Drain and serve with plenty of melted butter (quickly melted in the hot saucepan) poured over the cobs. Two forks or cocktail sticks will serve as corn-on-the-cob holders.

Sweetcorn is very good grilled on the barbecue, and served with lots of butter as before.

Frozen corn-on-the-cob is available all year – cook as directed on the packet.

SWEET POTATOES

A grubby-looking reddish 'potato', with the most beautiful yellow-pink flesh and a delicious sweet flavour. Best washed, then boiled or baked in its skin, peeled after cooking and mashed with butter. Sweet potatoes can also be roasted like roast potatoes (see page 96) or added to mixed roast potatoes. They can also be peeled thickly, cut into chunks and mashed with butter on their own or with potatoes, to make a delicious pink creamy mash.

TOMATOES

'Love apples' add colour and flavour to many dishes. They are used raw in salads or as a garnish, can be grilled or fried, chopped up and added to casseroles or stews, or stuffed as a supper dish. Choose firm tomatoes and keep them in the fridge for freshness. Cheaper soft tomatoes are a good buy for cooking, provided that you are going to use them straightaway.

Wash and dry the tomatoes, cut them into slices or quarters to use in a salad or a garnish. Tomatoes are easy to cut or slice thinly if you use a bread knife or a vegetable knife with a serrated edge. The skin will then cut more easily without the inside squidging out.

GRILLED
Cut them in half, dot with butter and grill for 3–5 minutes. Alternatively, put them in the grill pan under the grid when grilling sausages, bacon, chops or steak, as the tomatoes will then cook with the meat.

FRIED
Cut the tomatoes in half and fry them in a little oil or fat, on both sides, over a medium heat, for a few minutes until soft. Serve with bacon and sausages, or place on a slice of toast or fried bread.

BAKED
Heat the oven at 180°C/350°F/Fan 160°C/Gas Mark 4.

Cut a cross in the top of any small or medium sized tomatoes and halve any large ones. Put them into a greased, ovenproof dish or tin, with a knob of butter on top. Bake for 10–15 minutes until soft.

TURNIPS

Small white root vegetables, not to be confused with swedes.

Allow $1/_2$–2 turnips per serving, according to size and appetite.

Peel the turnips thickly. Leave small ones whole, but cut large turnips in half or quarters. Cook them in boiling water for 10 minutes until soft. Drain them well. Return the turnips to the pan and shake over a low heat for a few moments to dry them out. Serve with a knob of butter.

Turnips can also be served with one or two diced carrots. Just peel them and cut them into large dice, mix them with the carrots and boil them together for 5–10 minutes. Drain and dry as above.

Purée
Peel the turnips and cut them into chunks. Cook them in boiling water for 5–10 minutes until soft. Drain well, and dry as above. Mash with a fork or potato masher, with a knob of butter and some pepper.

AUBERGINE BAKE

Serves 1

A quick and easy-to-prepare lunch or supper dish, which can be eaten with potatoes and a green vegetable, or a salad and garlic bread or bread rolls. It can also be served as an accompaniment to meat or fish for a really substantial meal.

Takes 30 minutes

1 medium onion
1 medium aubergine
1 clove garlic or $1/_4$ tsp garlic powder (optional)
1 tbsp vegetable oil
1 small (225 g) tin tomatoes or half a big tin
1 tsp tomato purée or tomato ketchup
$1/_2$ tsp sugar
$1/_2$ tsp mixed herbs
Salt and black pepper
Few sprigs fresh parsley, coriander or chives
1 tbsp grated Cheddar or Parmesan cheese

Heat the oven at 200°C/400°F/Fan 180°C/Gas Mark 6.

Peel and chop the onion. Wash the aubergine, trim and cut into cubes. Peel and chop the fresh garlic.

Heat the oil in a pan over a moderate heat. Add the onion, aubergine and garlic and fry very gently for 10 minutes until soft. Chop the tomatoes and add to the pan with the tomato purée or ketchup. Stir in the sugar and season to taste with the mixed herbs, salt and pepper. Cook gently for a further 5 minutes, stirring carefully. Mix in fresh snipped parsley, coriander or chives and spoon the mixture into a greased ovenproof dish. Sprinkle with the grated cheese and bake in the hot oven for 10–15 minutes until the top is bubbling and golden brown.

BUBBLE AND SQUEAK

Serves 1

A good cheap and tasty meal, using up cold, leftover vegetables –
although you can cook some fresh veg specially if you wish. Serve
with cold meats, bacon, sausages or fried egg.

Takes 15 minutes

Leftover cooked potato
Leftover cooked cabbage and/or broccoli
These should be in the ratio of approximately 2 cups of
**   potato to 1 cup of cabbage – but exact measurements**
**   don't matter**
A little oil and a knob of butter (for frying)

Put the potato into a bowl and mash well. Add the cabbage
and/or broccoli and mash all together. Heat the oil and butter in
a frying pan over a medium heat, carefully tip in the potato mixture and smooth into a large, thick pancake shape or two small
cakes. Cook gently for 3–4 minutes, then turn the 'pancake' over
and cook the other side. When golden and crispy on both sides,
tip onto a warm plate and serve.

CRISPY CABBAGE CASSEROLE

Serves 1

This is filling enough to serve as a supper dish with hot bread
rolls, or goes well as an accompaniment with chicken.

Takes 35 minutes

$^1/_4$–$^1/_2$ a white cabbage (according to size)
1 small onion
1–2 sticks celery

2 tsp oil
1 thick slice white or brown bread
A little extra butter or spread for the topping

Cheese Sauce – or use a pack of sauce mix
2 tsp oil
150 ml/$^1/_4$ pint/1 cup milk
12 g/$^1/_2$ oz butter
25–50 g/1–2 oz grated Cheddar cheese

Heat the oven at 200°C/400°F/Fan 180°C/Gas Mark 6. Grease a deep ovenproof dish.

Trim the stalk and outer leaves from the cabbage. Shred it, not too finely, wash it well and drain. Peel and chop the onion. Wash and scrape the celery and cut into 2.5 cm/1 inch lengths.

Heat the oil in a frying pan over a moderate heat, and fry the onion for 2–3 minutes until soft but not browned. Add the celery and cabbage and fry for a further 5 minutes, stirring occasionally.

Make the cheese sauce (see page 228) or prepare the packet sauce according to the instructions.

Spoon the cabbage mixture into the greased dish and pour the cheese sauce over the top. Grate or crumble the bread into crumbs (or use a blender if you have one), and sprinkle the crumbs on top of the sauce.

Dot with the extra butter or spread, and bake in the hot oven for 15 minutes until the top is crunchy and golden brown.

MIXED ROAST VEGETABLES

Serves 2–3

Choose a good mixture of fruit and vegetables from the list below. Don't try to use all of them; you won't be able to cram them all into the roasting tin! However, the more vegetables you use, the more people you can feed, so it's a good dish to cook if you invite friends to dinner. Serve on its own with garlic bread and a salad, or serve as an accompaniment with meat or fish.

For a vegetarian main meal, add 100 g/4 oz diced halloumi cheese to the roasting vegetables for the last 15 minutes of cooking time.

Takes 1 hour 15 minutes
Use any mixture of vegetables according to taste and availability

2–3 medium onions (one for each person)
$^1/_2$ small swede
1 parsnip
2 medium potatoes
1 sweet potato
1–2 carrots
3–4 sticks celery
1 courgette
2–3 tomatoes
2–3 medium sized mushrooms
$^1/_2$ small pepper – any colour
1 crisp eating apple
1 or 2 fresh apricots or nectarines
3–4 tbsp olive oil or vegetable oil

Topping (optional)

1–2 tbsp salted peanuts or cashew nuts, roughly chopped

1–2 tbsp dried fruit – sultanas, seedless raisins, chopped apricots

$^1/_2$ tsp dried mixed herbs

Salt and black pepper

Few sprigs fresh parsley, chives or coriander, finely snipped

Heat the oven at 200°C/400°F/Fan 180°C/Gas Mark 6.

Prepare the vegetables and fruit according to type. Peel the onions, cut in half. Peel the root veg and cut into wedges, chunks or thick slices (different shapes look interesting!). Cut the celery into short lengths, and the courgette into chunks. Remove core or stones from the fruit, and cut into halves or quarters.

Heat a roasting tin, remove from the oven and put the prepared onion and root vegetables into the tin. Pour on the oil and mix well, coating all the pieces, spread into one layer and put in the oven. After 15 minutes mix in the rest of the fruit and vegetables, and cook for a further 35–40 minutes, until everything is golden and slightly crispy, but don't let them get too brown or over cooked.

Remove the veg and fruit from the tin onto a warmed serving dish, and serve at once or keep warm while you prepare the topping.

Topping

Put the nuts, dried fruit and dried herbs into the roasting tin with a little more oil if needed and season with salt and pepper. Return the tin to the oven for 2–3 minutes to warm through. Remove from the oven and carefully pour the topping over the warm vegetables. Garnish with fresh snipped herbs and serve.

RED CABBAGE CASSEROLE

Serves 1 main meal or 2 as a veg

Usually cooked in the oven to make a warming winter vegetable dish – good served with a jacket potato which can cook in the oven with the casserole. Can also be served as a vegetable accompaniment with meat or fish.

Takes 60–75 minutes

$^1/_2$ **small red cabbage**
2 tsp cooking oil
1 small onion – peeled and thinly sliced
1 eating apple – washed, cored and sliced with skin left on
Salt and black pepper
1–2 tsp brown or white sugar
1–2 tsp vinegar
$^1/_2$ **cup boiling water**
Small knob of butter

Cut off the cabbage stalk and remove any battered outside leaves. Shred the cabbage finely, rinse and drain.

Melt the oil in a small pan and fry the onion gently for 2–3 minutes until softened but not browned.

Oven Method
Heat the oven at 180°C/350°F/Fan 160°C/Gas Mark 4.

Use an ovenproof casserole dish with a lid, or a deep dish and cover with foil.

Put layers of the cabbage, apple and onion, seasoning each layer with a sprinkle of salt, pepper, sugar and vinegar, continuing the layers until all the vegetables are used up. Pour the boiling water over the vegetables, add a final sprinkle of sugar and dot with the butter.

Cover with the lid or foil and bake in the oven for about 1 hour.

Pan Method

Use a medium size saucepan, and put in layers of vegetables as in the oven method above. Pour on the boiling water, sprinkle with a little sugar and dot with butter. Put on the saucepan lid and simmer very gently for 45–50 minutes, until soft.

Serve hot.

> **QUICK TIP** *Any leftovers can be kept in the fridge and reheated for the next day's dinner.*

STUFFED MARROW

Eat one piece of marrow today and the other piece tomorrow, or invite a friend to share your supper. Serve with a jacket potato and a side salad.

Takes 1 hour

1 small marrow or a piece of a large one
1 small onion
2–3 mushrooms
A little oil and butter (for frying)
1 packet dried herb stuffing mix
2 tbsp grated cheese
Few sprigs fresh parsley if available

Heat the oven at 180°C/350°F/Fan 160°C/Gas Mark 4.

Cut the marrow in half lengthways, peel, scoop out and discard the seeds. Put the marrow in a pan and simmer in boiling water for 5–6 minutes until just beginning to soften – if the marrow is too long you will have to cut the pieces in half.

Remove from the pan with a slotted spoon (save the water) and put the marrow pieces into a greased ovenproof dish. Peel and finely chop the onion and fry gently in a small saucepan for 3–4 minutes.

Rinse, dry and coarsely chop the mushrooms, and fry with the onion for a further 2–3 minutes. Mix the packet stuffing as directed on the packet using the water in which the marrow was simmered and stir into the onion mixture.

Fill the pieces of marrow with the stuffing and top with the grated cheese. Cover the dish with cooking foil and bake for 30–40 minutes until the marrow is soft, removing the foil for the last 10 minutes to brown the cheese.

5

RICE, PASTA, NOODLES AND PORRIDGE

Rice is usually served as an accompaniment to curry, or with other main dishes instead of potatoes, although it is delicious cooked with meat or vegetables to make a creamy risotto.

It's best to serve rice when it has just been cooked to prevent any bacteria in it causing food poisoning. Therefore, time your rice to be cooked and ready to eat at the same time as the rest of the meal. (This should be quite easy, as rice takes only 20–30 minutes to cook, depending on the type of rice you are using.) If you have any leftover cooked rice, you should cool it as quickly as possible (ideally within one hour) and keep it in the fridge for no more than one day until reheating, making sure that the rice is really hot (not just warm) before serving. Alternatively, leftover cooked rice can be put into a plastic container and kept in the freezer to use at a later date; it freezes well and defrosts quickly. Fluff the defrosted rice with a fork to break up the lumps and use to thicken a casserole or in fried rice dishes, always making sure that the rice is thoroughly hot right through before serving.

Never leave cooked food of any kind standing out in the kitchen. Always put it into the fridge as soon as possible to prevent any bacteria multiplying and causing food poisoning.

Pasta and noodles can be cooked and served in lots of ways, plain with melted butter, cream or fromage frais and served instead of potatoes, or mixed with thick meat or vegetable sauces or cheese to make a meal on its own, with a green salad.

I didn't know where to put 'porridge' in this book, but my Scottish researcher is adamant that it ought to be included.

RICE
BOILED RICE

A good quick standby which saves peeling potatoes. Long grain (Patna or basmati rice) is used for savoury dishes as the grains stay separate when cooked. The smaller, 'stickier' round grain rice is used for puddings. Brown rice, whole unrefined rice, is also used for savoury dishes.

Rice is cheaper to buy in a large packet, and keeps for ages if kept covered and dry. You can buy 'easy cook' rice which should be cooked according to the instructions on the packet. This type of rice is very good, but it is usually more expensive than plain long grain rice.

When cooking rice, you can follow the exact instructions on the pack or use the general conventional methods below.

METHOD 1

Serves 1

I prefer this method, as I tend to let the pan boil dry with Method 2! However, you do need a largish pan and it's a bit steamy as the rice must be cooked without the lid on, otherwise it boils over.

Takes 12 minutes for white rice; 20 minutes for brown rice

50 g/2 oz/$^1/_2$ cup long grain rice (white or brown)
Water

Put the rice in a largish pan, fill the pan half full with boiling water and stir. Bring the pan back to the boil, reduce the heat and boil gently until the rice is cooked but still firm – see the times above. Don't overcook or the rice will go sticky. Drain well (easiest in a sieve, it may fall through a colander), fluff with a fork and serve.

Serves 1

Be careful that the rice doesn't boil dry.

Takes 13–16 minutes

1 tsp oil or small knob of butter
50 g/2 oz/¹/₂ cup long grain white rice
1 cup boiling water

Put the oil or butter in a smallish saucepan and heat gently. Add the rice, stirring all the time to coat each grain. Add the boiling water, bring up to simmering point and stir. Put on the lid and leave to simmer over a very gentle heat for 12–15 minutes. Test to see if the rice is cooked: all the liquid should be absorbed and the rice should be cooked but not soggy. Lightly fluff with a fork and serve.

MICROWAVE METHOD

Use 50 g/2 oz/¹/₂ cup of rice per serving and follow the instructions on the packet or in your microwave instruction book.

'Boil in the Bag' rice is not suitable for microwave cooking.

PILAU RICE

Serves 1

1 tsp cooking oil or butter
75 g/3 oz/³/₄ cup white basmati rice
A pinch of seeds and spices – cumin seeds, green cardamoms
1 cup of boiling water

Prepare Pilau rice as above in Method 2, stirring the spices with the rice in the hot oil or butter. Cook as above, and serve with cooked meat, fish or vegetables.

FRIED RICE

A good way of using up leftover boiled rice from the previous day.

Takes 15 minutes (plus 15 minutes if you have to boil the rice first)

1 cup cooked boiled rice (use $^1/_2$ cup raw rice)
$^1/_2$ onion or 1 salad onion
$^1/_2$ slice cooked, chopped ham (optional)
1 tbsp cooking oil
1 tbsp frozen peas and/or sweetcorn (optional)

Cook the rice if necessary (see page 116). Peel and chop the onion, or wash and chop the salad onion. Chop the ham.

Heat the oil in a frying pan over a medium heat. Add the chopped onion and fry, turning frequently, until soft. Add the cooked rice, and fry for 4–5 minutes, stirring all the time.

Add the frozen peas (still frozen; they will defrost in the pan), sweetcorn and ham, and cook for a further 2–3 minutes, stirring all the time, until it is all heated through.

You can make this more substantial by adding more vegetables and chopped cooked meat (ham, salami, garlic sausage, etc) if you wish.

EGG FRIED RICE

A popular accompaniment with curries.

Prepare the Fried Rice as opposite and leave in the pan.

Break an egg into a cup and beat well with a fork. Heat 1 tsp oil in another frying pan or small saucepan, pour in the egg and cook gently until set (like a little pancake). Tip the cooked egg onto a plate and cut into thin strips or small pieces and stir gently into the Fried Rice. Reheat the mixture and serve.

RISOTTO

Serves 1

A cheap meal if you have any 'pickings' of chicken left over. Or use a thick slice of cooked ham, chicken or turkey. It can be served with a green salad. (You don't need all the vegetables listed here; choose those you like.)

Takes 35 minutes

1 egg
1 small onion
1 tbsp oil
100 g/4 oz/1 cup raw white rice
1 stock cube and 300 ml/$^1/_2$ pint/2 cups boiling water
1 slice/25–50 g/1–2 oz cooked ham, chicken or turkey
2–3 mushrooms
1 tomato
1 tbsp frozen or canned peas
1 tbsp frozen or canned sweetcorn
Salt, pepper, Worcester sauce
25 g/1 oz grated Cheddar and Parmesan cheese (optional)

Hard boil the egg (see page 23). Peel and finely chop the onion.

Heat the oil in a medium saucepan or frying pan with a lid and fry the onion for 3–4 minutes until soft. Add the rice and fry, stirring well, for a further 3 minutes.

Dissolve the stock cube in the boiling water. Add this to the rice, stir and leave to simmer with the lid on, stirring occasionally, for 10–15 minutes, until the rice is tender, and the liquid almost absorbed.

Chop the meat. Peel and chop the hardboiled egg. Wash and slice the mushrooms. Wash and chop the tomato. Add the peas, sweet-corn, mushrooms and tomato to the rice. Cook for 2–3 minutes, stirring gently. Then add the chopped meat and egg, and continue stirring gently until heated right through. Season with salt, pepper and Worcester sauce. Serve with lots of grated cheese and/or Parmesan and a dash of Worcester sauce.

PASTA

Pasta is available dried and fresh. Dried pasta can be bought very cheaply in every supermarket and corner shop, while fresh pasta is more expensive (unless you have a pasta machine and make your own) and is sold in larger supermarkets and specialist shops. Dried pasta lasts for ages, so it is cheaper to buy a large packet if you eat pasta often.

There are numerous shapes of pasta, but they are all cooked in the same way, and most of the different shapes are interchangeable in most recipes – with the exception of lasagne and cannelloni types, and the very long spaghetti which some people like to cook unbroken so that they can twirl huge mouthfuls around their fork!

Spaghetti
Available in various lengths and thicknesses.

Tagliatelle and other Noodle varieties
Sold in strands and bunches.

Fancy shapes
Shells, bows, etc.

Macaroni types
Thicker tubular shapes

Lasagne
Large flat sheets

Cannelloni
Usually filled with a tasty stuffing.

Most makes of pasta have the cooking instructions on the packet, and the best advice is to follow these carefully.

DRIED PASTA

Allow approximately 75 g/3 oz/1 cup pasta per serving

Pasta must be cooked in a large pan of boiling water, with a few drops of cooking oil added to the water to help stop the pasta sticking.

Let the water come to the boil, add the pasta (long spaghetti is stood in the pan and pushed down gradually as it softens), then lower the heat and leave to simmer (without the lid on or it will boil over) for 8–10 minutes until the pasta is just cooked (*al dente*). Drain well, in a colander preferably or you risk losing the pasta down the sink. Serve at once.

FRESH PASTA

Fresh pasta should be cooked as dried pasta, but will only take 3–5 minutes to cook.

For a really quick and easy-to-prepare meal, buy fresh pasta and a carton of ready-to-use sauce (tomato, three cheese or any of the other delicious flavours available). Cook the pasta, heat the sauce and mix them together.

Fresh cannelloni, covered with a ready-to-use sauce and cooked in a hot oven (as instructed on the pasta pack) is absolutely delicious, served with hot garlic bread!

MACARONI CHEESE

Serves 1

This is traditionally made with the thick, tubular macaroni, but is just as good made with pasta shapes (shells, bows, twists, etc). Serve with a crisp green salad or cooked green vegetables.

Takes 30 minutes

$^1/_2$ tsp cooking oil
75 g/3 oz/1 cup macaroni or chosen pasta

Cheese sauce (or use packet mix)
2 tsp flour
150 ml/$^1/_4$ pint/1 cup milk
Large knob of butter
50 g/2 oz grated Cheddar cheese
Salt, pepper, $^1/_4$ tsp mustard

Topping
25 g/1 oz grated Cheddar cheese
1 sliced tomato (optional)

Heat the oven at 200°C/400°F/Fan 180°C/Gas Mark 6. Grease an ovenproof dish.

Half fill a largish pan with boiling water, add the cooking oil and pasta and boil gently for 10–15 minutes until just cooked (*al dente*).

While the macaroni is cooking, make the cheese sauce (see page 228) or make up the packet sauce.

Drain the macaroni well, and put into the dish. Pour the sauce over the macaroni, mix slightly and sprinkle the rest of the grated cheese over the sauce and top with the tomato slices.

Bake in the hot oven for 5–10 minutes until the cheese is crisp and bubbling and the macaroni has heated right through.

TRADITIONAL BOLOGNESE SAUCE

Serves 1

This thick meaty sauce can be used with spaghetti, pasta shapes, lasagne or even mashed potato, for a cheap and cheerful dinner.

Takes 45 minutes

1 small onion
$1/_2$ carrot
$1/_2$ rasher of bacon
Clove of garlic or pinch of garlic powder
2 tsp oil
75–100 g/3–4 oz minced beef
$1/_2$ small (230 g) tin of tomatoes or 2 fresh tomatoes
2 tsp tomato pureé or tomato ketchup
$1/_2$ beef stock cube and $1/_2$ cup of water or $1/_2$ small
   (295 g) tin of tomato soup
Pinch of salt and pepper
Pinch of sugar
Pinch of dried herbs

Peel and chop the onion. Peel and chop or grate the carrot. Chop the bacon. Peel, chop and crush the garlic clove.

Fry the onion and bacon gently in the oil in a saucepan, stirring until the onion is soft (2–3 minutes). Add the minced beef and continue cooking, stirring until it is lightly browned.

Add the carrot, tinned tomatoes (or chopped fresh ones), tomato purée (or ketchup), stock cube and water (or the soup), stirring well. Add the salt, pepper, sugar and herbs.

Bring to the boil, then lower the heat and simmer, stirring occasionally, for 20–30 minutes, until the meat is tender.

VERY EASY BOLOGNESE SAUCE

Serves 1

Couldn't be easier – a meal in 30 minutes.

Takes 30 minutes

2 tsp cooking oil
100 g/4 oz minced beef
1 small (198 g) jar Bolognese Cook-in Sauce

Heat the oil in a small saucepan over a moderate heat. Add the minced beef and fry for about 5 minutes until the meat is nicely browned.

Stir in the sauce, bring to a gentle boil, then reduce the heat and simmer gently for 20–25 minutes until the meat is cooked and ready to use.

If you cook 75 g/3 oz pasta (see page 123) while the sauce is cooking, your meal will then be ready to serve.

QUICK BOLOGNESE SAUCE

Serves 1

Very fast and easy to prepare. Use instead of Bolognese Sauce made with fresh minced beef.

Takes 10 minutes

1 small (198 g) tin minced steak
1 or 2 tomatoes (tinned or fresh)
2 tsp tomato purée (or tomato ketchup)
Pinch of garlic powder (optional)
Pinch of salt and pepper
Pinch of sugar
$^1/_2$ tsp dried herbs

Empty the minced steak into a saucepan. Chop the tinned or fresh tomatoes, add to the beef, with the tomato purée (or ketchup), garlic powder, salt, pepper, sugar and herbs. Bring gently to the boil, stirring well, then lower the heat and simmer for 5 minutes, stirring occasionally. Use as Traditional Bolognese Sauce.

VEGETABLE LASAGNE

Serves 1 or 2 according to appetite

A really tasty meal, and cheaper than lasagne made with meat.
Serve with a salad, hot garlic bread or bread rolls.

Takes 20 minutes to make the Vegetable Sauce
30 minutes to make and cook the Lasagne

1 medium onion – peeled and finely chopped
1 medium leek – cleaned, prepared and cut into rings
$^1/_2$ red or green pepper – washed and sliced
1 courgette – washed and cut into 0.5 cm/$^1/_4$ inch slices
1–2 sticks celery – washed and cut into 1 cm/$^1/_2$ inch
lengths
100 g/4 oz mushrooms – washed and sliced
1 small (230 g) can of tomatoes or 3–4 fresh tomatoes,
chopped, with $^1/_2$ cup of cold water
1 tbsp vegetable or olive oil (for frying)
$^1/_2$ tsp sugar
$^1/_2$ tsp dried mixed herbs
Dash of soy sauce

Cheese Sauce (page 228, 1 serving per person)
Or use a packet sauce and make according to the instructions, or
use half a tub of 'ready to use' sauce (but this is expensive!).

Extra cheese – 1–2 tbsp grated Cheddar to sprinkle over
the lasagne

Pasta – allow 3–4 lasagne strips per person

Prepare the vegetables (check the methods given earlier in this
section).

Heat the oil in a medium saucepan over a moderate heat, and fry the onion and leek for 3–4 minutes. Add the pepper, courgette, and celery, and fry for a further 3–4 minutes until just softened.

Add the mushrooms, stir in the tinned tomatoes and juice or chopped fresh tomatoes and water, sugar, herbs and soy sauce. Stir together gently and simmer for 8–10 minutes to make a 'sauce' consistency.

Heat the oven at 180°C/350°F/Fan 160°C/Gas Mark 4.

Assemble the lasagne: use a deep ovenproof dish, large enough for two helpings or an individual foil dish for one person. Put layers of the vegetable sauce, lasagne strips and cheese sauce into the dish and continue to alternate the layers, ending with the final layer of cheese sauce. Sprinkle with the grated cheese, and bake in the hot oven for 15–20 minutes until hot and the cheese is golden and bubbling.

The vegetable sauce can be used with spaghetti to make a 'Vegetable Spaghetti Bolognese' (see page 131) or mixed with most kinds of cooked pasta in an ovenproof dish, topped with grated cheese and cooked in a hot oven until the cheese is golden and bubbling.

BEEF LASAGNE

Serves 1 or 2 according to appetite

For this dish you can use the Traditional Bolognese Sauce or the Quick Bolognese Sauce. Serve with a healthy green salad and hot garlic bread or bread rolls if you're really hungry.

Takes 45 minutes if using Traditional Bolognese Sauce
or 10 minutes if using Quick Bolognese Sauce
5 minutes to make the Cheese Sauce
30 minutes to make the Lasagne

Traditional Bolognese Sauce (page 125, 1 serving per person) or
Quick Bolognese Sauce (page 127, 1 serving per person)

Cheese Sauce (page 228, 1 serving per person)
Or use a packet sauce and make according to the instructions, or use half a tub of 'ready to use' sauce (but this is expensive!).

Extra cheese – 1–2 tbsp grated Cheddar to sprinkle over the lasagne

Pasta – allow 3–4 lasagne strips per person

Prepare the chosen Bolognese Sauce.

Prepare the Cheese Sauce.

Heat the oven at 180°C/350°F/Fan 160°C/Gas Mark 4.

Assemble the lasagne: use a deep ovenproof dish, large enough for two helpings or an individual foil dish for one person. Put layers of the meat sauce, lasagne strips and cheese sauce into the dish and continue to alternate the layers, ending with the final layer of cheese sauce. Sprinkle with the grated cheese, and bake in the hot oven for 15–20 minutes until hot and the cheese is golden and bubbling.

SPAGHETTI BOLOGNESE

Serves 1

Grated Cheddar cheese can be used instead of Parmesan, but a drum of Parmesan keeps for ages in the fridge and goes a long way.

Takes 25–55 minutes

Traditional Bolognese Sauce (see page 125) or Quick Bolognese Sauce (see page 127)
75 g/3 oz spaghetti or 1 cup pasta shells, bows, etc
$^1/_2$ tsp cooking oil
2 tsp Parmesan cheese or 25 g/1 oz grated Cheddar cheese

Prepare the Bolognese Sauce.

Cook the spaghetti or chosen pasta in a pan of boiling water with $^1/_2$ tsp cooking oil for 10–12 minutes. (If you want to have long spaghetti, stand the bundle of spaghetti in the boiling water and, as it softens, coil it round into the water without breaking.)

Drain the spaghetti and put it onto a hot plate. Pour the sauce into the centre of the spaghetti and sprinkle the cheese on the top. Serve at once.

NOODLES

A really quick, cheap and cheerful meal. Serve on its own or with vegetables or a nice, big salad.

Takes 10–15 minutes

100 g/4 oz/1 big cup dried or fresh noodles – or adjust the amount to suit your appetite
1 tsp cooking oil or olive oil

Cook the noodles in a large saucepan of boiling water with the chosen cooking oil for 7–10 minutes (dried noodles) or 3–5 minutes (fresh noodles) or according to the instructions on the packet. Make sure you don't overcook them.

Prepare the 'sauce' while the noodles are cooking.

Drain the noodles, return to the hot, dry pan and shake for a moment in the pan over the heat to dry them.

Stir in the chosen 'sauce', pile into a warm dish and serve at once.

SAUCES

Butter and Salt
Stir 25–50 g/1–2 oz butter into the hot noodles, and season with a pinch of salt and black pepper.

Cheese
Grate 50 g/2 oz Cheddar or other hard, strong flavoured cheese and stir into the hot noodles with a large knob of butter.

Cheese and Chive
Mix a few finely snipped chives into the noodles with the cheese, and garnish with 3 or 4 green strands.

Tomato and Cheese
Slice and chop 2 or 3 tomatoes and add with the cheese and butter as above.

Carbonara
Chop or slice 2–3 slices of cooked ham and stir into the hot noodles with 25 g/1 oz butter.

Pesto
Stir 2–3 tbsp pesto sauce into the hot noodles with a knob of butter if liked.

Blue Cheese
Crumble up 50 g/2 oz blue Stilton or other blue veined cheese and stir into the hot noodles.

Cheese and Walnut
Add 1 tbsp broken walnuts with the cheese – especially tasty with blue cheese.

These are just a few suggestions. Mix some of the 'sauces' together – Cheese and Pesto, Carbonara with Tomato and Cheese – or use your own favourite ingredients.

STIR FRY WITH SWEET AND SOUR SAUCE

Serves 1 or 2

A really quick meal to make. All the fruit and vegetables are shredded or finely chopped, and then fried quickly in a wok or frying pan. Stir in sweet and sour sauce (or a sauce of your choice) and serve at once with ribbon noodles. You can save time by using a pack of 'stir fry vegetables', available in lots of different mixtures from most supermarkets.

Takes 15–30 minutes

Choose a good selection of vegetables but include some onion
1 small onion
1 carrot
75–100 g/3–4 oz mushrooms
5 cm/2 inch piece cucumber or small courgette
$^1/_2$ small red pepper and $^1/_2$ small green pepper
1 or 2 eating apples
A few sugar snap peas (leave whole)
1 cup of beansprouts
1 cup shredded Pak Choi
1 tbsp vegetable or olive oil
1–2 tbsp cashew nuts and/or peanuts and/or pine nut kernels
1–2 tsp soy sauce or Sweet and Sour Sauce
   (see recipe opposite)

Prepare your vegetable selection and shred, slice or chop into even sized pieces.

Heat the oil in a wok or large frying pan, add the vegetables and fry for 5–10 minutes until softened but still crunchy.

Stir in your chosen sauce, tip onto a serving plate and serve at once.

Sweet and Sour Sauce

2 tsp flour

1 tbsp sugar

1 tsp soy sauce

2 tbsp vinegar

1 tsp vegetable stock powder or $^1/_2$ stock cube dissolved in $^1/_2$ cup of boiling water

Put the flour and sugar into a small saucepan and mix to a smooth paste with the soy sauce and vinegar. Stir the hot stock into the mixture and simmer over a moderate heat, stirring all the time, until the sauce thickens and becomes transparent.

Serve with noodles – see page 132

Allow 100 g/4 oz dried or fresh noodles per serving or use 'instant cook' noodles and follow instructions on the packet

Beef or Chicken Stir Fry

Use 75–100 g/3–4 oz raw steak or chicken breast per person

Before cooking the vegetables, cut the beef or chicken into thin strips and fry in the pan for 4–5 minutes. Remove from the pan and cook the vegetables. Return the meat to the pan with the vegetables before stirring in the sauce and serve at once.

PORRIDGE

1 good Scottish serving

A good warm, filling start to the day, or a cosy bedtime snack – and you don't *have* to sprinkle it with salt! You can make it really delicious, and extra good for you, by adding Demerara sugar, honey, golden syrup, raisins or other dried fruit, chopped apples, dates or nuts, when the porridge is cooked, or topping it with fresh fruit – cranberries, blueberries, raspberries, sliced strawberries, peaches, bananas or any other favourite fruit. And, of course, to be really wicked, top with cream!

Takes 4–6 minutes

40 g/1^1/$_2$ oz/^{1}/$_2$ cup of porridge oats
1 cup of water, milk or a mixture
Any extras as listed above

Put the oats, milk and/or water in a small saucepan and bring to the boil over a moderate heat, stirring gently. Reduce the heat and simmer gently for 4–5 minutes until the porridge is thick and creamy, still stirring gently. Add the extras and serve.

Porridge can also be cooked in the microwave. Follow the instructions on the porridge oats packet or in your own microwave book, but always cook the porridge in a LARGE bowl as the porridge will rise up the bowl while cooking in the microwave.

6
BACON, SAUSAGES, HAM AND OTHER QUICK MEATY DISHES

Lots of 'quick to cook' but substantial dishes in this section, so that you can soon have a good hot meal ready to eat when you arrive home tired and hungry.

BACON

Serve 2–3 rashers per person

Streaky bacon rashers are smaller and cheaper, while back bacon and gammon are the most expensive. How well cooked you like your bacon is a very personal thing: I know someone who likes hers cremated! As a rough guide: cook for between 1–5 minutes. Tomatoes and/or mushrooms can be cooked in the grill pan under the rashers of bacon; the fat from the bacon will give them a good flavour.

Cut off the bacon rinds if you wish or just snip the rinds at intervals.

GRILLED

Heat the grill. Put the bacon on the grid in the grill pan and cook, turning occasionally, until it is cooked to your taste.

FRIED

Heat a smear of oil or fat in a frying pan. Add the bacon and fry over a medium-hot heat, turning occasionally, until the bacon is as you like it.

SAUSAGES

These come in all shapes, sizes and pieces; the thicker the sausage, the long it takes to cook. Have you tried eating sausages with marmalade? I'm told it is delicious, and a boarding school speciality.

Cook as many sausages as you can eat. Cook with a gentle heat to stop the sausages bursting.

GRILLED

Heat the grill. Put the sausages on the grid in the grill pan, and cook, turning occasionally, until brown and delicious (about 10–20 minutes). Thicker sausages may brown on the outside before the middle is cooked, so turn the heat down to medium for the last 5–10 minutes of cooking time.

FRIED

Heat a smear of oil or fat in a frying pan over a medium heat (too hot a pan will make the sausages burst their skins), add the sausages and fry gently, turning occasionally, until they are brown and crispy (10–20 minutes). Cook thick sausages for the longer time, using a lower heat if the outsides start getting too brown.

ROAST

Heat the oven at 200°C/400°F/Fan 180°C/Gas Mark 6.

Roast chipolata (thin) sausages are traditionally served as accompaniments to roast turkey and chicken. Roasting is an easy way of cooking sausages if you're not in a hurry. Place the sausages in a lightly greased tin and bake in the hot oven, turning occasionally to cook all over, until crisp and brown (15–25 minutes). Thicker sausages take the longer time.

A PROPER BREAKFAST

Serves 1

Tastes just as good for lunch or supper.

Takes 20 minutes

Use any combination of ingredients according to taste and appetite

1–2 rashers of bacon – streaky or back
1 tomato
3–4 mushrooms
1–2 leftover cold boiled potatoes
1–4 sausages
1 tbsp oil (for frying)
2–3 tbsp baked beans
1–2 eggs
1 slice of bread (for fried bread)
Knob of butter
Several slices of bread (for toast)

The breakfast, apart from the eggs, potatoes and fried bread which are better fried, can be grilled if you prefer. Get everything ready before you actually start cooking: de-rind the bacon, wash and halve the tomato, wash the mushrooms and slice the potatoes. Warm a plate, put the kettle on ready for tea or coffee, get the bread ready to make the toast, and you're all set to start. In both methods, start cooking the sausages first, as they take the longest to cook, gradually adding the rest of the ingredients to the pan.

FRYING

Heat the oil in a frying pan over a moderate heat and fry the sausages gently, turning occasionally, allowing 10–20 minutes for them to cook according to size. When the sausages are half cooked, put the bacon in the pan with them and fry for 1–5 minutes with the sausages, until they are cooked to your taste. Push the sausages and bacon to one side or remove and keep warm. Put the potato slices into the pan and fry until crispy. Fry the tomato and mushrooms at the same time, turning them occasionally until cooked (about 4–5 minutes). Put the baked beans in a small pan and heat gently.

Remove the food from the pan and keep hot. Break the eggs into a cup, and slide them into the hot fat in the pan over a low heat. Fry them gently until cooked (see page 25). Remove them from the pan and put them with the bacon, sausages, etc. Cut the slice of bread in half, and fry in the fat in the pan, adding a little extra oil or butter if necessary, until golden and crispy, turning to cook both sides (1–2 minutes). Remove from the pan and put onto the plate with the rest of the breakfast. Make the toast, coffee or tea, and eat at once.

GRILLING – THE HEALTHY 'GOOD FOR YOU' METHOD

Heat the grill. Put the tomato halves and mushrooms in the base of the grill pan, arrange the sausages above on the grid, and grill until half cooked (5–10 minutes), turning to cook on all sides. Arrange the bacon on the grid with the sausages, and continue cooking for a further 3–5 minutes, turning to cook both sides. Remove everything from the pan and keep it warm. Put the baked beans in a small pan and heat gently. Pour the fat from the grill pan into a frying pan, add extra oil or butter if necessary, then fry the potato slices, eggs and fried bread as described above, and enjoy it all with lots of toast, marmalade, and lovely strong coffee or tea.

BANGERS AND MASH AND ONION GRAVY

Serves 1

Fast, filling, cheap and very tasty.

Takes 30–40 minutes

2–3 potatoes – according to size and appetite
2–4 sausages – according to size and appetite
Knob of butter
1–2 tsp cooking oil (for frying the sausages)

Gravy
1 smallish onion
2 tsp cooking oil and/or a little butter
1 tsp flour and 1 tsp gravy flavouring powder or 2 tsp
**   gravy granules**
$1/_2$ stock cube or $1/_2$ tsp stock powder (pork or chicken)
1 cup of water from the cooked potatoes or plain water

First start to make the gravy
Peel and finely slice the onion. Heat the oil or butter in a small pan, stir in the onion slices and fry gently for 5–10 minutes until lightly brown and soft, stirring occasionally.

While the onions are frying
Peel the potatoes, cut into even-sized pieces, put into a pan and cook in gently boiling water for 10–15 minutes until soft.

Fry or grill the sausages (see page 139) until brown, and keep them warm until needed.

Test the potatoes with a fork and, if soft, drain the cooked potatoes in a sieve or colander over a basin or jug (to save the water) and mash the potatoes with a masher or fork, beating in the knob of butter. Keep the potatoes warm.

Finish the gravy
Put the flour and gravy flavouring powder, or gravy granules, and crumbled stock cube, or stock powder, into a basin and mix to a smooth paste with a little cold water. Pour into the cooked onions, stirring well and gradually adding about 1 cup of the saved potato water. Continue to cook and stir over a gentle heat until the gravy thickens, adding any juices from the cooked sausages.

Pile the mashed potato onto a plate, arrange the sausages round it and pour the delicious oniony gravy over the sausages.

TOAD IN THE HOLE

Serves 1

You can use either large sausages (toads) or chipolatas (frogs) for this meal, whichever you prefer! Some people believe that a better Yorkshire Pudding is made if the ingredients are mixed together first and the batter is then left to stand in the fridge while you prepare the rest of the meal. Alternatively, make the batter while the sausages are cooking.

Takes 45–55 minutes

3–6 sausages (according to appetite and size)
1 tbsp cooking oil

Yorkshire Pudding batter
2 heaped tbsp plain flour
Pinch of salt
1 egg
150 ml/$^1/_4$ pint/1 cup milk

Heat the oven at 220°C/425°F/Fan 200°C/Gas Mark 7.

Put the sausages into a baking tin with the oil. (Any baking tin can be used but not one with a loose base. You do not get as good a result with a pyrex-type dish.) Cook chipolatas for 5 minutes, larger ones for 10 minutes.

Make the batter while the sausages are cooking. Put the flour and salt in a basin, add the egg, and beat it into the flour, gradually adding the milk, to make a smooth batter. (This is easier with a hand or electric mixer, but with a bit of old-fashioned effort you can get just as good a result using a whisk, wooden spoon or even a fork.)

Pour the batter into the baking tin on top of the hot sausages. Bake for a further 20–25 minutes, until the Yorkshire Pud is golden. Try not to open the oven door for the first 10–15 minutes, so that the pudding will rise well.

Serve at once.

SAUSAGE AND BACON HUBBLE BUBBLE

Serves 1

A tasty way of using up odds and ends from the fridge.

Takes 30 minutes

2–3 cooked boiled potatoes
1 small onion
1 rasher of bacon
2 tsp oil (for frying)
2–4 sausages
1 egg
55 ml/2 fl oz/ $^{1}/_{2}$ small cup of milk
Salt and pepper

Heat the oven at 190°C/375°F/Fan 170°C/Gas Mark 5.

Grease an ovenproof dish.

Slice the cooked potatoes. Peel and chop the onion. De-rind the bacon.

Heat the oil in a frying pan, and fry the sausages, bacon and onion gently for 5 minutes, turning frequently.

Place the potato slices in the dish. Arrange the onions, sausages and bacon on top. Beat the egg with the milk, salt and pepper in a small basin, using a whisk or fork. Pour the egg mixture over the top, and bake in the hot oven for about 15 minutes, until the egg mixture is set.

FRIED LIVER AND BACON
WITH FRIED ONIONS

Serves 1

I know that lots of people 'don't like liver' but for the *sensible* ones who do here is a quick and easy recipe for a really tasty, cheap meal – why not try it and see?! Eat with nice hot crusty bread or hot garlic bread, or baked beans; a big green side salad would add a healthy touch!

If you want to make a more substantial meal, serve with a jacket or mashed potato and some green vegetables – broccoli, French or runner beans or frozen peas are nice. You could also make onion gravy (see page 142) instead of the plain fried onions.

Takes 15–20 minutes

2–3 tsp cooking oil
1 smallish onion – peeled and sliced
1–2 rashers bacon
2–3 slices lamb's liver (liver shrinks a bit as it cooks)
Knob of butter

Heat 2 tsp oil in a frying pan over a gentle heat, add the sliced onion and fry for 4–5 minutes, stirring frequently until soft. Push to one side of the pan.

Add a little more oil to the pan if needed, and carefully put the bacon and liver into the pan, turning often until cooked to taste – liver should be soft on the outside and pale pink inside when cut, so try not to over cook it or it will become grey, tough and tasteless.

Remove the liver and bacon from the pan onto a warm plate, spoon on the fried onions and pour the juices from the pan over the liver and bacon.

FARMHOUSE SUPPER

Serves 1

A tasty quick-to-prepare brunch, lunch or supper.

Takes 20–30 minutes

1 small slice of raw gammon or 2 bacon rashers
3 tsp cooking oil
3–4 cooked boiled potatoes (see page 94) – diced
1 small onion – peeled and thinly sliced
2 or 3 medium size mushrooms – washed and sliced
1 medium tomato – washed and sliced thickly
1 or 2 eggs
25 g/1 oz grated cheese

De-rind the gammon or bacon and cut into strips. Heat 1 tsp oil in a frying pan over a moderate heat, and lightly fry the gammon or bacon for 3–4 minutes. Remove from the pan and put aside.

Add a little more oil to the pan and fry the diced potatoes and onion for 5–6 minutes until the onion is soft and the potatoes lightly brown. Mix in the sliced mushrooms and tomato, and cook for a few more minutes until they are soft.

Mix the gammon or bacon into the vegetables and spoon into a greased ovenproof dish.

Add a little more oil to the frying pan if needed, and fry 1 or 2 eggs (according to appetite).

Turn the grill on to heat while the eggs are cooking.

Carefully slide the cooked eggs on top of the vegetables and gammon or bacon, cover with the grated cheese and brown for a few moments under the hot grill until the cheese is bubbly. Serve at once.

KEBABS

Kebabs can be cooked under the grill, but are much nicer barbe-
cued outside with friends. You can get a better variety of meat if
you are serving more people, as each kebab only requires one or
two pieces of each type of meat, so a small piece of steak would
cut into enough pieces for several kebabs, and packets of ready
prepared assorted meat for kebabs are available at the supermarket. Try to put a good mixture of meat and vegetables on each
skewer.

Serve with boiled rice or rice salad (see pages 116 or 68), jacket
potatoes, coleslaw, potato salad or green salad, garlic bread or
bread rolls, and, of course, barbecue sauce and tomato ketchup.

Takes 20–30 minutes

Allow at least 1–2 skewers per person

2–3 rashers bacon
2–3 chipolata sausages
1 small thick piece rump steak }
1 small thick pork steak   } one kind of meat is fine
1 small thick piece gammon   }
8–12 button mushrooms
6–12 small tomatoes
1 green, red or yellow pepper
1–2 onions
A few pineapple cubes if liked
Oil for brushing
1–2 long skewers for each person

Prepare boiled rice, salads, potatoes and bread before starting to cook the kebabs.

If barbecuing, remember to light it in plenty of time to get it hot.

Assemble and prepare your chosen ingredients as follows:

De-rind the bacon, cut the rashers in half to make them shorter and roll them into little bacon rolls. Twist and halve the sausages. Cut the rump steak, pork steak or gammon into 2 cm/1 inch cubes. Wash and dry the mushrooms and tomatoes. Wash and dry the peppers, slice into chunks. Peel the onions and cut into quarters. Drain the pineapple cubes (drink the juice).

Thread a good mixture of the prepared food onto the skewers, arranging it according to taste. Brush or wipe the kebabs with a little cooking oil.

Cook on the barbecue or under a moderate grill, on the grill rack, for about 10 minutes, turning carefully to cook both sides. Serve the kebabs on the skewers – they will be hot, so provide paper napkins or have kitchen paper handy.

Kebabs can be cooked balanced across a baking tin in a hot oven (200°C/400°F/Fan 180°C/Gas Mark 6) for 10–15 minutes.

HAGGIS, NEEPS AND TATTIES

Serves 2–3 or more

Celebrate Burns' Night or St Andrew's Day with this traditional Scottish fare. It's not as difficult as it sounds, as good, ready-to-cook haggis is available at most large supermarkets and butcher's shops at the appropriate times of year, ready to heat in the oven or steam.

Traditionally, Haggis is served with Neeps (mashed swede) and Crabbit Tatties (mashed potatoes), and – if you're old enough – the haggis is accompanied with a tot of whisky!

Takes about 1 hour, depending on how big a haggis you're cooking

1 ready-to-cook haggis (a small one serves 2–3 people)
1 medium-large swede
700 g/1¹/₂ lb potatoes or according to appetite

COOKING THE HAGGIS

The ready-to-cook haggis is pre-cooked, so you only have to heat it through really thoroughly and serve piping hot. Buy the size suitable for the number of people it must feed, and follow the instructions for cooking on the packet.

Baking: Heat the oven at 180°C/350°F/Fan 160°C/Gas Mark 4. Wrap the haggis loosely in foil in case it should split and place it in an ovenproof casserole dish with a little water. Cover the dish and cook in the oven for 45 minutes.

Boiling: Wrap in foil as above, put in a saucepan, just cover with boiling water and cook in the gently boiling water for 45 minutes, topping up the pan with boiling water if needed.

Microwaving: Follow the instructions on the pack or in your microwave book – but do not wrap in foil.

Time the vegetables to be ready when the haggis is cooked.

COOKING THE NEEPS

Peel the swede thickly, so that no brown or green skin remains, and cut into 1.25 cm/$^1/_2$ inch dice. Cook in a large pan of gently boiling water for about 20 minutes, until soft.

Drain well in a colander, return the swede to the pan and mash with a potato masher (or a fork, but that's hard work), to make a smooth purée, adding a large knob of butter and black pepper. Put into a serving dish and keep warm until ready to eat.

COOKING THE TATTIES

Peel the potatoes, removing any black bits. Cut into thick slices and cook in a large pan of gently boiling water for 10–15 minutes until soft – do not let them overcook or fall to bits in the water. Drain well in a colander, return the potatoes to the pan and mash well with a potato masher or fork until fluffy. Pile onto a serving dish and keep warm until needed.

Put the haggis onto a serving dish, remove the foil and carry the haggis whole to the table. Serve hot with the neeps and tatties.

NB Very tasty VEGETARIAN HAGGIS is also available, and may be preferred by the more squeamish, besides the vegetarians!

LUNCHEON MEAT PATTIES

Serves 1

Cheap and tasty, and filling enough for lunch or supper if served with fried eggs. Or simply serve with fresh or fried tomatoes.

Takes 20 minutes

3–4 potatoes
1 small onion
100 g/4 oz luncheon meat (canned or sliced)
A little beaten egg
Salt and pepper
Pinch of dried herbs
Oil (for frying)
Knob of butter (for frying)

Peel and thickly slice the potatoes. Cook them in boiling water for 10 minutes until soft. Drain them and mash well.

Peel and finely chop or grate the onion. Chop the luncheon meat.

Mix together the potato, onion and luncheon meat, and bind with the well–beaten egg, adding sufficient egg to hold it all together. Season with the salt, pepper and herbs. Form the mixture into 3 or 4 equal portions. Shape each into a ball and then flatten to form 'beefburger' shapes about 2 cm/$^3/_4$ inch thick.

Heat the oil and butter in a frying pan, and fry over a moderate heat for 3–5 minutes, turning to cook both sides, until crisp and golden brown.

SAVOURY CORNED BEEF HASH

Serves 1

Every cowboy's favourite standby!

Takes 30 minutes

3–4 potatoes
$^1/_2$ small onion
50–100 g/2–4 oz corned beef
Salt and pepper
1 tbsp oil (for frying)
1 egg
1 tsp tomato purée (or ketchup)
1 tbsp hot water
A dash of Worcester sauce
A dash of tabasco sauce

Peel the potatoes, cut into large dice, and cook for 5–6 minutes in boiling water until half cooked. Drain well.

Peel and finely chop the onion. Dice the corned beef. Mix together the potato cubes, onion and corned beef. Season with salt and pepper. Well grease a frying pan with oil and put the meat and potato mixture into the pan.

Beat the egg. Dissolve the tomato purée or ketchup in 1 tbsp of hot water, beat this into the egg, add the Worcester and tabasco sauces, then pour onto the meat mixture. Fry gently for about 15 minutes, stirring occasionally. Serve hot.

I have known people to make this gourmet dish using cooked rice instead of cooked potatoes, but it has not been particularly successful.

GAMMON STEAK WITH PINEAPPLE OR FRIED EGG

Serves 1

Buy a thick slice (1.25 cm/$^1/_2$ inch at least) of gammon, if possible as thin slices just go crispy like bacon. Serve with boiled new potatoes and salad in summer and sauté or jacket potatoes and peas in winter.

Takes 6–10 minutes according to taste

1 steak or slice (about 175 g/6 oz) gammon
Little oil
1–2 tinned pineapple rings or 1 egg

GRILLED

Heat the grill. Snip the gammon rind at intervals. Brush or wipe both sides of the gammon with a smear of oil. Place the gammon on the grid of the grill pan and cook each side under the hot grill for 3–5 minutes, until brown. Put the pineapple slices on top of the gammon and heat for a few moments or fry the egg in a frying pan, in a little hot fat. Serve the gammon with the pineapple slices or with the egg on top.

FRIED

Snip the gammon rind at intervals. Heat a smear of oil or fat in a frying pan. Add the gammon and cook each side for 3–5 minutes until brown. Add the pineapple rings to the pan and heat for a few moments or fry the egg in the hot fat. Serve the gammon with the pineapple rings or with the egg on top.

7

FISH DISHES

Fresh fish is available at most larger supermarkets, market and seaside fish stalls, travelling fish vans and the (rapidly disappearing) fishmonger's shops. Very good frozen fish is widely available, both as fish to prepare yourself as part of a meal, and as ready-to-heat main meals. Also frozen fish is generally a little cheaper than fresh fish.

When buying fresh fish, look for the 'special offers of the day', as they are often very good value, and ask the fishmonger how to prepare the fish if you are unsure how to cook it – most people are only too pleased to give advice, and a good fishmonger will fillet and prepare the fish for cooking if necessary. Most pre-packed fish will have cooking instructions on the packet.

Fresh fish should be stored in the fridge, and is best cooked and eaten on the day it is bought. Frozen fish must be defrosted and cooked on the same day, and should *never* be refrozen after defrosting.

FISH AND CHIPS

There are lots of ready-to-cook packs of fresh or frozen fish in batter or breadcrumbs, and so many makes, sorts, sizes and flavours of oven ready chips, just waiting to be quickly cooked in a hot oven, that I'm sure everyone can easily treat themselves to a delicious meal of fish and chips, following the instructions on the packet, served with tinned mushy peas, vinegar and tomato ketchup.

Or, what about a nice fillet of fish, with freshly cooked chips and mushy peas from the chip shop!

FRIED FISH FILLETS
IN LEMON BUTTER

Serves 1

Serve with new potatoes, boiled or jacket potatoes and a fresh green salad, fresh green beans or frozen peas.

Takes 15–20 minutes

**175–225 g/6–8 oz fillet of white fish (fresh or defrosted) –
    haddock, cod and plaice are among the cheaper fish
25–50 g/1–2 oz butter
1 tsp cooking oil
Thick slice of lemon or 1 tsp lemon juice
Snipped parsley (optional)
Extra slice of lemon (optional)**

Prepare the chosen potatoes and salad or vegetables.

Wash and dry the fish on kitchen paper.

Melt the butter with the oil in a frying pan (the oil stops the butter going too brown), over a moderate heat. Carefully add the fish fillet and fry until tender (about 5–10 minutes), spooning the melted butter over the fish as it cooks. *Be careful not to overcook the fish or it will be dry and break easily; the thinner the fillet, the quicker it will cook.*

Lift the fish carefully onto a warm plate and keep warm.

Squeeze the thick slice of lemon into the pan, or add the lemon juice, and stir to make a lemony sauce. Pour the sauce over the fish, sprinkle with snipped parsley, garnish with the extra slice of lemon and serve at once.

QUICK TIP *Fresh or frozen ready prepared fillets of cod, haddock or plaice in breadcrumbs or batter are widely available and can be fried or baked in the oven as you prefer. To cook: follow the instructions on the packet and serve with chips or boiled potatoes in butter and/or a side salad.*

PRAWN COCKTAIL

Serves 2

Sounds quite decadent and is fun to serve if you have a guest. It's quick and easy to prepare and looks much more interesting than prawn salad. Halve the quantities if just 'cooking' for one. Serve the cocktails in large wine glasses with thin slices of brown bread and butter.

Takes 15 minutes

2–3 tbsp mayonnaise
$1/_2$ tsp tomato ketchup
75–100 g/3–4 oz shelled prawns (fresh or defrosted)
4–5 crisp lettuce leaves – Cos or Iceberg type or mixed
**   leaves if you prefer**
2 thin slices of lemon, cut from the middle of a lemon
**   so that they are quite large**
Paprika for garnish

Put the mayonnaise in a small basin or cup and gradually mix in enough tomato ketchup to make a *pale* pink sauce.

Rinse and drain the prawns, making sure that frozen prawns are thoroughly defrosted. Put them into a small basin and stir in 1 tbsp sauce, coating the prawns lightly.

Wash and dry the chosen lettuce and shred finely. Put some lettuce in each wine glass, and then layer prawns and lettuce alternately, ending with some prawns on the top. Spoon the rest of the sauce over the two cocktails.

Cut the lemon slices from the centre to the edge, and twist one over the rim of each glass and garnish with a sprinkle of paprika over the sauce.

Keep in the fridge until ready to eat.

GRILLED TUNA STEAK

Serves 1

As tuna is a rich oily fish, it is best served with plain boiled rice, or new or boiled potatoes and green vegetables – broccoli, French beans, runner beans, etc.

Takes 10 minutes

**175–225 g/6–8 oz tuna steak – at least 2 cm/$^1/_2$ inch
   thick so that the fish does not dry up during cooking
Oil for brushing
Thick slice of lemon**

Prepare and cook the chosen vegetables, etc, and keep warm.

Turn on the grill to get hot.

Wipe the fish with damp kitchen paper, and brush or wipe with a little cooking oil.

Put under the hot grill and grill for 2–3 minutes on each side – do not overcook as the fish will then taste dry. The fish should be just pale pink inside when cooked, although some people prefer rare tuna, like rare beef.

Serve at once with the prepared vegetables.

FRIED TUNA STEAK

Tuna steaks can also be fried in a pan with a little oil and butter, over a moderate heat. Be careful not to cook the fish too quickly over too high a heat, as the outside will get hard and dry before the inside of the fish is cooked.

TOMATO FISH BAKE

Serves 1

Buy a thick piece of cod or haddock fillet to cook in the oven with a delicious tomato sauce. Serve hot, with vegetables, salad or crusty bread.

Takes 35 minutes

175–225 g/6–8 oz thick piece cod or haddock fillet
$^1/_2$ small onion
$^1/_2$ small can (230 g size) tomatoes or use 2 large fresh tomatoes
Small piece green or red pepper (optional)
1 stick celery (optional)
2 tsp cooking oil
2 tsp tomato purée or ketchup
Salt and black pepper
Pinch of garlic powder
Pinch of dried mixed herbs
Few sprigs fresh parsley, washed and finely snipped

Heat the oven at 190°C/375°F/Fan 170°C/Gas Mark 5.

Rinse the fish and put into a greased ovenproof dish.

Peel and chop the onion. Chop the fresh tomatoes, pepper and celery.

Heat the oil in a small saucepan, add the chopped onion and fry gently for 2–3 minutes until soft.

Add the tinned or chopped tomatoes, chopped pepper and celery, stir in the tomato purée or tomato ketchup, and simmer gently for 3– 5 minutes, adding a little water if necessary, to produce a thick sauce. Season the sauce with salt, pepper, garlic, herbs and parsley, and pour over the fish.

Cover the dish with a lid or cooking foil, and bake for 15–20 minutes in the hot oven.

> **QUICK TIP** *You could use a small jar or carton of 'ready to use' tomato sauce if you prefer. Just pour it over the fish and cook as above.*

FRIED OR GRILLED TROUT
OR MACKEREL

Serves 1

Fresh trout can be bought quite cheaply from trout farms or supermarkets, etc; frozen trout is good value too. Mackerel is also widely available and both fish can be cooked in the same way.

Serve hot with a slice of lemon or a drop of vinegar, accompanied by lots of fresh bread and butter for a cheap and filling meal. Alternatively, serve with new potatoes and a mixed green salad if you want to be more elegant and healthy!

When you buy fresh fish, ask the fishmonger to clean and prepare the fish for cooking. Frozen fish is already cleaned.

Takes 15 minutes

1 tsp oil (for frying)
Knob of butter
1 trout or mackerel
Slice of lemon (optional)
Vinegar (optional)

To Fry

Heat the oil and butter in a frying pan over a moderate heat, carefully slide in the fish and fry over a gentle heat for 3–4 minutes on each side (depending on the size of the fish) until done.

To Grill

Heat the grill. Brush the fish with oil and/or dot with butter and grill for 3–4 minutes on each side (depending on the size of the fish) until cooked.

To Microwave

Trout and mackerel also cook well in the microwave oven.
Put the prepared fish in a greased cooking dish and slit the fish two or three times on each side to prevent it bursting. Brush with oil or dot with butter, cover the dish and cook on full power for 2 minutes. Turn the fish over and cook for a further 2 minutes.
Check the cooking instructions for your own microwave oven as they may vary.

SMOKED HADDOCK WITH POACHED EGG

Serves 1

This makes a good, quick lunch or supper, served with creamy mashed potatoes, or, as a real treat, cook for a lazy Sunday breakfast, and eat with warm muffins, bread rolls or toast.

Takes 30 minutes

150–225 g/6–8 oz smoked haddock fillet
Knob of butter
Black pepper
About 1 cup milk
1 egg

Heat the oven at 180°C/350°F/Fan 160°C/Gas Mark 4.

Grease a deep pie dish or ovenproof dish, and put in the fish. Dot with butter and season with black pepper. (This fish doesn't need salt due to its smoky taste.) Pour the milk over the fish but don't cover it completely. Bake in the moderate oven, without a lid, for 15–20 minutes.

Prepare a clean frying pan and hot water ready to poach the egg. When the fish is almost cooked, poach the egg (see page 24).

Use a fish slice to put the haddock onto a plate, then carefully top with the poached egg and serve at once with your chosen accompaniments.

QUICK TUNA SUPPER

Serves 1

A really quick 'store cupboard' supper. Serve with plain boiled rice for an almost instant hot meal.

Takes 25 minutes

75 g/3 oz/³/₄ cup long grain white rice
1–2 tsp cooking oil
1 small onion – peeled and finely chopped
¹/₂ clove garlic or a pinch of garlic powder
50 g/2 oz mushrooms – washed and sliced
¹/₂ small pepper – any colour – washed and chopped
3 tbsp frozen or drained tinned peas
3 tbsp drained tinned sweetcorn kernels
2–3 tbsp tinned tomato soup
¹/₂ can (200 g size) tuna fish – or more according to appetite – store the rest in the fridge and use for sandwiches
Few sprigs parsley or coriander – washed and finely chopped

Put the rice on to cook – see page 116.

Heat the oil in a saucepan over a moderate heat, add the onion and garlic and fry gently for 4–5 minutes until soft but not browned.

Stir in the sliced mushrooms and chopped pepper, and continue to fry gently for a further 2–3 minutes. Add the peas (frozen peas will defrost and cook in the mixture), sweetcorn and tomato soup, and stir gently for a few more minutes until the mixture is hot.

Add the tuna in chunks, stirring very carefully so that the fish does not break up into tiny pieces, and cook for a few minutes to warm right through.

Drain the rice, fluff with a fork and spoon it onto a plate to form a deep ring. Spoon or pour the tuna mixture into the middle, and sprinkle with chopped parsley or coriander if available.

TASTY FISH PIE

Serves 1

Use any fresh or frozen fillet of white fish, according to what is the best buy – cod, coley, haddock are all suitable; other fish is usually more expensive. Fresh or frozen prawns, hard boiled egg and the creamy rich potato topping make it really delicious.

Takes about an hour

Topping
2 or 3 potatoes (according to appetite)
Large knob of butter
Grated nutmeg
1 tbsp fresh cream, crème fraîche or creamy milk

175 g/6 oz white fish fillet
2 tsp flour
About 150 ml/$^1/_4$ pint/1 cup milk
25 g/1 oz butter
1 hard boiled egg, peeled and sliced (see page 23)
About 25 g/1 oz peeled prawns (fresh or defrosted)
Salt and pepper

Heat the oven at 200°C/400°F/Fan 180°C/Gas Mark 6.

Peel the potatoes, cut into thick slices and cook in gently boiling water for 10–15 minutes.

Grease a deep ovenproof dish, put in the fish. Dot with butter and pour over enough milk to almost cover the fish. Bake in the oven for 10 minutes.

Drain the potatoes when cooked, and mash with a potato masher or fork until smooth. Beat in the butter, season with a pinch of grated nutmeg and beat in the cream, crème fraîche or creamy milk. Put the lid on the pan until the potato is needed.

When the fish is cooked, remove it from the dish onto a large plate, saving the milk from the fish for a sauce. Remove the skin and any bones from the fish, and break the fish into bite sized pieces.

Make a thick sauce – put the flour into a small pan and mix to a smooth paste with the milk from the fish, adding a little more milk to make a runny mixture. Cook the sauce over a moderate heat, stirring all the time, until the sauce thickens, adding more milk as needed. Beat in the butter and season with salt and pepper.

Spoon the fish pieces into the dish, add the hard boiled egg and prawns, and gently mix them all into the sauce, trying not to break the pieces. Cover carefully with the creamed potato, fork flat and bake in the hot oven for 10–15 minutes until crispy and golden.

OVEN COOKED FILLET OF SALMON

Serves 1

Salmon is now one of our cheaper and most popular fish. The fillets can be baked in the oven or cooked in the microwave, and are superb eaten with little new potatoes, fresh asparagus and a mixed green salad, or green beans, broccoli or frozen peas. Serve with Hollandaise sauce or a good mayonnaise.

Takes 15–20 minutes (plus time to prepare and cook potatoes, vegetables and sauce)

175–225 g/6–8 oz salmon fillet, fresh or defrosted
25 g/1 oz butter
Few sprigs watercress or parsley to garnish
Carton of ready to use Hollandaise sauce or jar of mayonnaise

Prepare and cook chosen vegetables.

OVEN METHOD

Heat the oven at 200°C/400°F/Fan 180°C/Gas Mark 6.

Put the salmon into a greased shallow ovenproof dish. Cover with a lid or foil, and bake in the hot oven for 15 minutes until tender.

MICROWAVE METHOD

Put the salmon into a microwave dish, cover with a lid or cling film, and cook on high for 2–3 minutes. *Check the cooking instructions for your own microwave oven as they may vary.*

Remove the salmon from the oven onto a serving plate, garnish with watercress or parsley and serve with chosen vegetables and Hollandaise sauce or mayonnaise.

QUICK TIP *Cooked salmon can be served cold. Keep it in the fridge until needed, then serve garnished with thin cucumber slices and mayonnaise, accompanied by little new potatoes and mixed green salad.*

8
CHICKEN DISHES

There is currently much debate about free range and organic chicken versus chicken produced by cheaper methods. Obviously the way chicken is produced is reflected in its price, and it is up to each individual to buy what his or her conscience dictates and what can be afforded.

Fresh and frozen chicken (a whole chicken, chicken joints, bone in or boneless, and chicken breast fillets) are extremely good value. There is very little waste (only the bones) and any scraps can be eaten cold or used up in sandwiches, risotto or fried rice.

Frozen chicken must be thoroughly defrosted before you start cooking, either by using a microwave (take care: thinner pieces don't start to cook at the edges), or by leaving the chicken in the packet at room temperature for several hours according to the pack instructions. You can hurry defrosting a little by putting the pack in a bowl of *cold (not hot)* water to melt the ice crystals, but chicken defrosted too quickly in hot water will be tough when cooked. If chicken is not thawed before cooking, it may not cook right through and any bacteria present won't be destroyed so could make you ill.

Chicken must be cooked thoroughly too. The juices should run clear, not tinged with pink, when pierced with a knife at the thickest part of the joint.

Instructions for thawing and cooking a whole roast chicken can be found in 'Sunday Lunch' Dishes, page 215.

There are lots of delicious ready prepared chicken dishes available at supermarkets, both chilled and frozen, which must be defrosted and cooked strictly according to the instructions on the packet.

Serve your cooked chicken with potatoes, oven chips, plain or fried rice, couscous, pasta or noodles, salad or your favourite vegetables.

Chicken joints on the bone (breast or leg) are best roasted rather than fried, as they may burn on the outside before the centre is cooked. They can be roasted and served in the same way as fried boneless chicken fillets in any of the recipes in this section. See also the recipe for Roast Chicken Pieces, opposite.

ROAST CHICKEN PIECES

Serves 1

An economical roast dinner for one. The chicken pieces are cooked in a roasting tin in the oven in the same way as a whole chicken, and can be served with stuffing, sausages, apple sauce, roast potatoes and vegetables to make a proper roast dinner.

Takes 45 minutes (plus defrosting time)

¹/₄ chicken or 1 or 2 chicken pieces – fresh or defrosted
2–3 tsp cooking oil
1 tsp dried mixed herbs (optional)

Heat the oven at 200°C/400°F/Fan 180°C/Gas Mark 6.

Brush or rub the chicken with oil, sprinkle with herbs (if used) and place in an oiled roasting tin. Cover the tin with cooking foil and roast for 30–40 minutes according to the size of the pieces, until the juices run clear (not pink) when tested with a pointed knife. (If still pink, cook for a few more minutes.) Remove the foil for the last 10 minutes of the cooking time to brown the chicken.

Chipolata sausages, roast potatoes and parsnips can be cooked round the chicken (see 'Sunday Lunch' Roast Chicken, page 218).

Remove the chicken, sausages and vegetables from the tin on to a serving plate and keep warm. Use the juices left in the roasting tin to make the gravy (see page 226).

PARTY CHICKEN DRUMSTICKS
For a party, buy chicken drumsticks (usually available in a 'party size' box) and cook in a large roasting tin as above, for 20–30 minutes, according to size. When cooked (test as above), remove from the roasting tin, allow to cool, and keep in a container in the fridge until ready to serve.

FRIED CHICKEN

Serves 1

A quick and easy dinner, served with potatoes and vegetables, or just eaten with crusty bread and butter and a salad.

Takes 20–25 minutes (plus defrosting time)

1 chicken breast fillet
Pinch of dried herbs (optional)
2 tsp oil and a little butter (for frying)

Defrost the chicken (see page 167) if frozen.

Wash the chicken, dry on kitchen paper and sprinkle herbs (if used) over both sides of the chicken.

Heat the oil and butter in a frying pan over a moderate heat. Add the chicken and fry gently for 15–20 minutes according to size, turning occasionally so that it browns on both sides. If the chicken seems to be getting too brown, lower the heat, but continue cooking as the chicken needs to cook right through.

Test with a pointed knife (any juices should be clear not pink). Remove the chicken from the pan onto a serving plate, pour over the juices from the pan if you wish, and eat hot or cold.

If you prefer you can roast a chicken breast or leg joint on the bone (see page 169) and serve as above.

CHICKEN IN TOMATO AND MUSHROOM SAUCE

Serves 1

Fried chicken breast in a tasty sauce. Serve with pasta or noodles.

Takes 35 minutes (plus defrosting time)

1 boneless chicken breast fillet or 175 g/6 oz chicken pieces
3 tsp cooking oil
$^1/_2$ small onion – peeled and chopped
2–3 mushrooms – washed and sliced
$^1/_2$ chicken stock cube or 1 tsp stock powder
100 g/4 oz/about 1 cup chopped tomatoes ($^1/_4$ of a 400g can)
1 tsp tomato purée or tomato ketchup
Pinch of dried mixed herbs
$^1/_2$ tsp sugar

Defrost the chicken thoroughly if frozen (see page 167). Cut the chicken into bite-sized chunks or cubes.

Heat 2 tsp oil in a frying pan over a moderate heat, and fry the chicken pieces for about 10 minutes, stirring occasionally, until browned on all sides.

Add a little more oil to the pan, add the onion and fry gently for 2–3 minutes to soften. Stir in the sliced mushrooms.

Crumble the stock cube or powder into the chopped tomatoes, and stir into the frying pan, mixing well so that the stock dissolves. Mix in the tomato purée or ketchup, herbs and sugar, bring to the boil, then reduce the heat and leave to simmer for a further 10 minutes, until the sauce is nice and thick, and the chicken pieces are cooked right through. Serve hot with cooked pasta or noodles.

CHICKEN WITH SWEETCORN

Serves 2

The sweetcorn and potato sauce turns the chicken into a complete meal, served perhaps with carrots or a green vegetable. You can roast chicken breasts or legs on the bone if you prefer for this dish – see page 169.

This recipe makes enough for two servings, as a very small quantity of sauce will dry up during cooking. Either invite a friend to dinner, or put the spare portion in the fridge for tomorrow or in the freezer for another day.

Takes 30 minutes (plus defrosting time)

2 chicken breast fillets
3 tsp oil and a knob of butter (for frying)
1 medium onion
1 can (329 g size) new potatoes
$^1/_2$ can (329 g size) sweetcorn kernels
25 g/1 oz butter
2 tsp flour
About 150 ml/5 fl oz/1 cup milk
50 g/2 oz salted peanuts
Salt and pepper

Defrost the chicken thoroughly if frozen (see page 167).

Melt the oil and butter in a frying pan over a moderate heat, add the chicken and fry gently for 15–20 minutes, turning occasionally until cooked and golden brown (see page 170). Or roast the chicken joints in the oven (see page 169).

Make the sauce while the chicken is cooking
Peel and chop the onion. Drain the potatoes and sweetcorn. Melt the butter in a small pan over a moderate heat, and fry the onion gently for 2–3 minutes. Add the potatoes and cook for a further 5 minutes, stirring gently. Mix in the sweetcorn.

Stir in the flour and cook for 1–2 minutes. Draw the pan off the heat and gradually stir in the milk. Return to the heat and bring slowly to the boil, stirring as the sauce thickens, adding a little extra milk if the sauce is too thick.

Add the peanuts and simmer for a few more minutes, stirring gently, being careful not to break up the potatoes. Season to taste. Put the chicken on a warm serving dish, cover the sauce and serve at once.

CHICKEN IN WINE (OR CIDER OR APPLE JUICE)

Serves 2

This can be made with chicken joints on the bone, but I prefer to use boneless chicken breast if possible. This recipe makes enough for two meals, so that the sauce does not dry up while cooking. The sauce is delicious made with white wine, but you can use cider or apple juice if you prefer.

Takes 45–60 minutes (plus defrosting time); chicken on the bone takes the longest time

2 chicken joints, breasts or legs, or boneless chicken breast fillets (175–225 g/6–8 oz each)
1 medium onion
1 eating apple
1 tsp oil and knob of butter
1–2 wine glasses white wine, cider or apple juice
2 tsp flour
1 stock cube or 2 tsp stock powder – preferably chicken flavour
About 150 ml/5 fl oz/1 cup hot water
1 tsp dried mixed herbs
Salt and pepper

Defrost the chicken if frozen (see page 167).

Peel and finely chop the onion. Peel, core and chop the apple.

Heat the oil and butter in a thick saucepan or casserole over a moderate heat, and fry the chicken gently for a few minutes, turning it so that it browns on all sides. Add the chopped onion and apple, and stir over a gentle heat for a few minutes to soften.

Pour the wine, cider or apple juice into the pan with the chicken, onions and apple, stir well and allow to bubble gently.

Mix the flour to a smooth, runny paste with a little cold water, in a basin, dissolve the stock cube or powder in a cup of hot water, and gradually stir or whisk the stock into the flour mixture, stirring to make a smooth sauce.

Pour the sauce over the chicken and stir in the dried herbs. Cover the pan and simmer *very gently* for 30–45 minutes, until the chicken is tender.

Mix the flour to a smooth runny paste with a little cold water, and mix it gradually into the chicken sauce, stirring gently until the sauce thickens, adding extra water if needed. Taste and season with salt and pepper and serve nice and hot.

HOISIN CHICKEN STIR FRY

Serves 1

Make up your own 'stir fry mixture' to cook with the chicken, using thinly sliced onion, peppers, carrots, pak choi, bean sprouts, mushrooms and a little fresh ginger, or any other Chinese style vegetables that you like, cut into thin, quick-to-cook pieces – or you can buy a bag of fresh, ready-to-use Stir Fry Chinese Vegetables from the wide variety available at most supermarkets and add your own favourite vegetables as extras.

Serve the stir fry with rice for a quickly prepared lunch or supper, or pile some of the cooked chicken and stir fry vegetables into a wrap or baguette for a quick 'lunch to go'.

Takes 15–30 minutes

1 raw chicken breast fillet
Mixture of fresh Chinese type salad vegetables, as above, prepared and thinly sliced
Or half a bag of ready prepared Chinese stir fry vegetables
1–2 tbsp oil (for frying)
1–2 tbsp Hoisin sauce
75 g/3 oz/³/₄ cup rice

Slice the chicken into strips 6–7 cm/2–3 inches long, or leave whole if you prefer.

Prepare a good mixture of thinly sliced raw salad vegetables.

Put the rice on to cook – see page 116.

Heat a little of the oil in a wok or frying pan, add the chicken strips or the whole chicken fillet and fry over a gentle heat for 5–6 minutes (strips) or 15–20 minutes (whole fillet).

Remove the chicken from the pan while you fry the vegetables. Turn the heat up to moderate, add a little more oil to the pan, tip in the chosen prepared vegetables, and fry for 4–5 minutes, stirring and turning the vegetables until they are cooked but still nice and crisp.

Return the chicken to the pan and stir in the Hoisin sauce and mix gently, coating the chicken and all the stir fry evenly.

Drain the rice and put onto a serving plate, spooning the chicken and vegetable mixture over the top.

If serving 'to go', fill a wrap, warm pitta bread or a baguette with the chicken mixture and eat while hot.

HOISIN BEEF STIR FRY

Use about 75–100 g/3–4 oz raw steak per person. Cut the steak into strips, and cook instead of the chicken strips as above.

HAWAIIAN CHICKEN

Serves 1

Cook half the tin of pineapple with the chicken, then eat the rest
for pudding, with ice-cream, cream or yogurt. Serve the Hawaiian
chicken with new or sauté potatoes, or potato castles, and green
beans or peas.

Takes 40 minutes (plus defrosting time)

1 chicken joint (175–225 g/6–8 oz)
1 tsp oil and knob of butter (for cooking)
$^1/_2$ small can (220 g size) pineapple pieces, chunks or
   slices in syrup or juice
1 tsp flour
1 tsp soy sauce
1 tsp Worcester sauce

Defrost the chicken, if frozen, for several hours at room temperature (see page 167).

Heat the oil and butter in a frying pan, and fry the chicken over
a moderate heat for 10 minutes, turning occasionally so that it
browns on all sides. Remove from the pan for a few minutes.

Drain the pineapple, saving the liquid. Mix the flour into a
smooth paste with a little of this liquid. Add the remainder of the
liquid and stir this mixture into the juices in the frying pan, stirring until the sauce thickens. Return the chicken to the pan, add
the pineapple pieces, and pour the soy sauce and Worcester sauce
over the chicken. Stir well, then lower the heat and simmer for 5
minutes, stirring occasionally. Serve nice and hot.

9
LOTS OF BEEF

Beef is generally one of the most expensive meats, especially if you buy meat for roasting or steak for grilling or frying, but it's nice to have the occasional treat! However, stewing steak and mince are much cheaper and can be made into delicious meals, although they do take longer to prepare and cook, as the cheaper the cut of meat, the longer the cooking time.

Stewing steak cooked in gravy needs cooking for $1^1/_2$–2 hours, so make enough for at least two helpings, as small amounts dry up before the meat is cooked, and check how much each recipe makes before you buy the ingredients.

BEEF CASSEROLE OR STEW

Serves 2

You can use any mixture of beef and (mainly) root vegetables to make a casserole (cooked in the oven) or a stew (simmered in a covered pan on top of the stove), so just combine the vegetables that you like. If you want the meal to go further, add extra vegetables, or if you're watching the pennies use less meat. You can buy packets of mixed root vegetables especially for casseroles, which are useful as you only need a small amount of each vegetable, and the more different types you use, the more interesting the meal.

Stews and casseroles are easier to cook in larger quantities, as small amounts tend to dry up during cooking, so this recipe is for two helpings. But why not double or triple the ingredients when you have a party, and serve with jacket potatoes cooked in the oven with the casserole – entertaining couldn't be easier and everyone will be very impressed!

Takes 2–2¹/₂ hours

1–2 tbsp oil (for frying)
1 onion – peeled and sliced
1 clove garlic (optional) – peeled and squashed
225–275 g/8–10 oz stewing steak – cut into 2.5 cm/1 inch cubes
1 beef stock cube
1 wine glass red wine or beer (optional) or water

Vegetables – any mixture according to taste
1–2 carrots – peeled and sliced
**Piece of swede (or small turnip) – peeled thickly, cut
    into 2.5 cm/1 inch chunks**
2 sticks celery – washed and cut into 2.5 cm/1 inch lengths
1 courgette – washed and cut into 2.5 cm/1 inch slices
¹/₂ aubergine – washed and cut into 2.5 cm/1 inch chunks
1 or 2 potatoes – peeled and cut into 2.5 cm/1 inch chunks

50 g/2 oz mushrooms – washed, dried and sliced if large
300 ml/¹/₂ pint water
¹/₂ tsp dried herbs
Salt and pepper

For thicker gravy
2 tsp flour and 1 tsp gravy flavouring powder
Or 4 tsp gravy granules
A little wine, beer or water to mix

For a casserole: Heat the oven at 170°C/325°F/Fan 150°C/Gas Mark 3.

Heat the oil in a heavy saucepan or casserole, add the onion and garlic (if used) and fry gently for 2–3 minutes until softened. Add the cubed meat and fry until brown, stirring so that it cooks evenly. Crumble the stock cube and stir into the meat with the wine, beer or water.

Add the chosen and prepared vegetables to the meat, adding enough water to almost cover the meat and vegetables. Add the herbs, bring slowly to the boil and stir well.

Then either put the covered casserole in the middle of the moderate oven, or lower the heat and leave the stew to simmer with the lid on the pan for 1¹/₂–2 hours, stirring occasionally. If it seems to be drying up, stir in a little more wine, beer or water.

Casseroles cook very well in a microwave on a low setting, usually for about half the cooking time of a conventional oven. Prepare the casserole in a pan on the stove as above, and transfer the meat mixture to a microwave dish to cook, and check the cooking instructions for your microwave.

If you like the gravy thicker, mix the flour and gravy flavouring powder or gravy granules with a little wine, beer or water to make a thin, runny paste, and stir it into the gravy in the dish for the last half hour of cooking. Taste the gravy carefully, adjust the seasoning, stir and serve bubbling hot.

COTTAGE PIE

Serves 1

A real favourite, even better than school dinners. The optional cheese in the potato makes a lovely tasty topping. The meat mixture can also be served on its own, and eaten with potatoes or rice or pasta or noodles and vegetables.

Takes 55 minutes

2 tsp oil (for frying)
1 small onion – peeled and chopped
1 clove garlic – peeled and squashed or pinch of garlic powder (optional)
100–150 g/4–6 oz minced beef
$1/2$ wine glass red wine or beer (if you have any opened)
1 large tomato – washed and chopped – or 1–2 tinned tomatoes
1–2 tsp tomato ketchup
Shake of Worcester sauce
$1/2$ stock cube (crumbled) or 1 tsp stock powder
1 smallish cup water or juice from tinned tomatoes
Pinch of mixed dried herbs

Topping
2–3 potatoes
25 g/1 oz butter, plus a little for the top of the pie
25–50 g/1–2 oz grated Cheddar cheese (optional)
1 tomato – sliced (optional)

Heat the oil in a saucepan, add the onion and garlic (if used) and fry gently for 2–3 minutes to soften. Add the minced meat and continue to fry, stirring all the time, until the meat is browned, about 2–3 minutes.

Stir in all the rest of the ingredients, adding enough water to make a runny mixture. Bring to the boil, then reduce the heat and leave to simmer for 20–30 minutes until the meat is tender – adding extra water while cooking if the mixture gets too dry.

While the meat is cooking, peel the potatoes and prepare as creamy mashed potatoes (see page 95). Stir in half the cheese (if used), saving enough for the topping.

Heat the oven if used at 200°C/400°F/Fan 180°C/Gas Mark 6.

Pour the hot meat mixture into an ovenproof dish, cover with the creamy mashed potato and fork down smoothly. Sprinkle the remaining cheese on top, or top with tomato slices and dot with butter.

Put the pie under a hot grill for a minute or two, watching carefully until the top is brown. Or, *if you don't have a grill,* cook the pie on the top shelf of the hot oven for 5–10 minutes, until golden brown.

BEEF CURRY

Serves 2

A change from the Indian take-away, and fun to make as you can vary the spiciness to suit your taste. This is a medium hot curry, and will make two helpings as small amounts dry up during cooking. Or why not double the ingredients for a party? Serve with plain or fried rice – see page 116 – poppadums and some side dishes, as below.

Takes about 2 ¹/₂ hours

1 tbsp cooking oil
1 onion – peeled and chopped
350 g/12 oz lean stewing beef – cut into 2.5 cm/1 inch cubes
2–3 tsp curry powder*
1 apple – washed, cored and chopped (no need to peel)
2 tomatoes – washed and chopped
1 small (295 g size) can mulligatawny soup
Or 1 beef stock cube dissolved in 200 ml/6 fl oz/
    1¹/₂ cups hot water
1 tbsp sultanas – washed and drained
2 tsp sugar
1 tbsp tomato chutney or brown pickle
*or you may prefer to mix your own curry paste

Heat the oil in a medium size saucepan over a moderate heat, and fry the chopped onion for 2–3 minutes to soften. Add the beef and fry for a further 5 minutes, stirring and turning the meat until it is browned all over.

Sprinkle the curry powder or chosen spices over the meat and stir for a few moments over the heat. Add the chopped apple and tomato and pour in the mulligatawny soup or stock. Stir in the sultanas, sugar and chutney or pickle, and mix well.

Bring to the boil, then lower the heat and simmer gently, with the lid on, stirring occasionally, for about 2 hours, adding a little more water if the curry seems too dry, until the meat is tender. Serve hot with chosen accompaniments.

CHICKEN CURRY

Use 2 fresh or defrosted chicken leg or breast joints

Prepare the curry using the recipe given opposite for beef curry, but using a small (295 g) can of chicken and vegetable soup or stock made with a chicken stock cube instead of beef stock, and adding 1 tbsp mango or tomato chutney instead of pickle. Chicken cooks quicker than beef, so the chicken joints will only need to simmer for about 1 hour until cooked as above.

SIDE DISHES FOR CURRIES

Salted nuts
Chopped green peppers
Plain yogurt
Sliced onions
Sliced banana (sprinkle with lemon juice to keep it white)
Chopped apple (sprinkle with lemon juice to keep it white)
Chopped cucumber
Chopped hardboiled egg
Washed, drained sultanas
Mango chutney
Desiccated coconut

POPPADUMS

Great fun to cook. Buy a packet of Indian poppadums, on sale at large supermarkets.

Heat 3–4 tbsp cooking oil in a frying pan over a medium heat (enough to cover the base of the pan). When the oil is hot, float a poppadum on top and it will puff up immediately, only taking a few moments to cook. Remove it carefully and leave it to drain on kitchen paper while cooking the next poppadum. Do not let the fat get too hot or it will get smoky and burn.

STUFFED PEPPERS

Serves 1 or 2 according to appetite

Lovely fresh, brightly coloured peppers are available in most supermarkets all year round. Choose one or two nice, big, well-shaped peppers for this dish. Serve with chips or hot French bread and butter.

Takes about 1 hour

1 tbsp cooking oil
1 small onion – peeled and chopped
100 g/4 oz minced beef
1 tomato – washed and chopped
1 tsp tomato purée or ketchup
$^1/_2$ stock cube or 1 tsp stock powder
75 ml/3 fl oz/$^1/_2$ cup boiling water
Shake of Worcester or soy sauce
Salt and pepper
Pinch of mixed dried herbs
1 tbsp long grain white rice
1 or 2 peppers – red, orange, yellow or green

Heat the oil in a saucepan over a moderate heat, and fry the onion for 2–3 minutes to soften. Add the minced beef and fry for a further 2–3 minutes until the meat is browned, stirring frequently. Stir in the chopped tomato and tomato purée or ketchup.

Dissolve the stock cube or powder in the boiling water and add to the meat mixture, with the Worcester or soy sauce, salt, pepper and herbs. Bring the mixture to a simmer, stir in the rice and continue to cook for 15–20 minutes, stirring occasionally. The stock should be almost absorbed but add a little more water if it gets too dry before the meat is cooked.

Heat the oven at 180°C/350°F/Fan 160°C/Gas Mark 4.

Grease a small ovenproof dish, big enough to hold the peppers. Cut the tops off the peppers (and keep them aside), remove the seeds, rinse the peppers and stand them in the prepared dish.

Take the meat mixture off the heat and carefully fill the peppers, straining off any excess liquid (the mixture wants to be moist but not swimming in gravy) and put the tops back on. Bake in the moderate oven for 20–30 minutes, until the peppers are soft.

BOEUF STROGANOFF

Serves 2

Absolutely delicious, slightly expensive (though less than serving steaks for two) and very impressive if you have a special friend to dinner. Traditionally served with plain boiled rice and a fresh green salad but good with noodles or new potatoes if preferred.

Takes 30 minutes

225 g/8 oz good rump steak, or fillet if you feel rich!
1 medium onion
1 clove garlic or garlic powder
100–150 g/4–6 oz mushrooms
1 small green or red pepper
100 g/4 oz/1 full cup long grain rice
1 tbsp cooking oil and 25 g/1 oz butter
Small carton (142 ml size) crème fraîche or double cream
Chopped parsley

Cut the steak into thin strips about 5 cm long by 1 cm wide (2 inches long by ¹/₂ inch wide), removing any fat or gristle. Peel the onion and slice into very thin rings. Peel and chop the fresh garlic. Wash, dry and slice the mushrooms. Wash the pepper, remove the core and seeds, and cut into strips.

Put the rice on to cook (see page 116) before you start cooking the stroganoff.

Put half the oil and butter into a large frying pan and melt over a moderate heat. Put the onion and garlic in the pan and fry gently for 3–4 minutes until soft. Add the mushrooms and pepper, and continue frying for a further 5–6 minutes until the vegetables are soft. Remove all the veg from the pan into a bowl while you cook the meat.

Melt the remaining oil and butter in the pan, turn up the heat a little to cook the meat quickly, add the steak strips to the pan and fry for 3–4 minutes, turning frequently so that they cook evenly. Do not over cook unless you prefer well done steak.

Return all the cooked vegetables and any juices to the pan and reheat thoroughly over a moderate heat. Gently stir in half the crème fraîche or double cream but *do not* let the sauce boil.

Drain the rice, and arrange around the edges of two plates to form a deep ring. Spoon the stroganoff into the centre of each ring, putting a good mix of meat and vegetables on each plate. Dribble the remaining crème fraîche or double cream over each plate, and sprinkle with chopped parsley. Serve at once.

HOMEMADE BEEFBURGERS

Serves 1

These are quite a change from the commercially produced beef-burgers. You can make them bun-sized or 'half-pounders'. Buy a good quality mince, as finely chopped as possible.

Serve in soft bread rolls (these are traditionally lightly toasted on one side) with tomato or barbecue sauce, or with potatoes, vegetables or a salad.

Takes 20–25 minutes according to size

$^1/_2$ small onion
125–225 g/4–8 oz minced beef, according to appetite
Salt and pepper
Pinch of dried herbs
Worcester (or tabasco) sauce
Little beaten egg (or egg yolk)
Little oil (for frying)

Peel and finely chop the onion, and mix well in a bowl with the minced beef, using a fork. Mix in the salt, pepper, herbs and sauce, and bind together with a little egg. The mixture should be wet enough so the ingredients mould together, but not soggy. Divide this into two portions, shape each into a ball, and then flatten into a circle, about 2 cm/$^3/_4$ inch thick.

Heat the oil in a frying pan over a medium heat. Put the beef-burgers carefully in the pan and fry for 10–15 minutes, according to size, turning occasionally to cook both sides. Do not have the heat too high as the beefburgers need to cook right through to the middle without burning the outside.

CHILLI CON CARNE

Serves 2

As small amounts dry up during cooking, this recipe makes enough for two servings. You can freeze one helping or keep it in the fridge for tomorrow. It's very good poured over a big jacket potato or served with plain boiled rice.

Takes 1 hour

1 medium onion
1 clove garlic or a little garlic powder
2–3 tsp cooking oil
225 g/8 oz minced beef
$^1/_2$ tsp chilli powder and/or few drops hot pepper sauce
1 beef stock cube or 2 tsp stock powder
About 250 ml/$^1/_2$ pint/2 cups hot water
1 tbsp tomato purée or ketchup
1 small (213 g size) cooked red kidney beans
2–3 tbsp crème fraîche

Peel and chop the onion, peel and squash the garlic clove. Heat the oil in a saucepan over a moderate heat, add the onion and garlic and fry until soft (3–4 minutes).

Add the mince and fry until brown, stirring so that it cooks evenly. Stir in the chilli powder and/or pepper sauce, crumble in the stock cube or powder, and mix with half the water. Add the tomato purée or ketchup, stir well and bring to the boil, adding more water as needed. Reduce the heat, cover the pan and simmer for 30 minutes, stirring occasionally, and adding a little more liquid if it gets too dry.

Stir in the drained kidney beans and simmer for a further 10 minutes to heat right through.

Taste *carefully(!)* and add more hot pepper sauce if liked. Serve hot, topped with a spoonful of crème fraîche.

HUNGARIAN STYLE GOULASH

Serves 2

A really quick and easy 'one pot' meal, as the potatoes are cooked in with the meat, and although it needs a longish cooking time (about $1^1/_2$–$1^3/_4$ hours), it can be left to cook in the oven without needing much attention while you are busy.

Takes 2 hours

2–3 tsp cooking oil
2 medium onions – peeled and sliced
250–300 g/8–10 oz stewing steak – cut into 4 cm/
** $1^1/_2$ inch cubes**
2 tsp paprika pepper
$^1/_2$ (400 g size) can chopped tomatoes
1 beef stock cube or 2 tsp stock powder
300 ml/$^1/_2$ pint/2 cups boiling water
1 tbsp tomato purée or ketchup
225 g/8 oz potatoes
50 g/2 oz mushrooms
2–3 tbsp crème fraîche

Cook the goulash on top of the stove in a heavy saucepan or flameproof casserole.

Heat the oil in the chosen pan over a moderate heat, add the onions and meat and fry gently, stirring to brown the meat on all sides.

Stir in the paprika and mix into the meat. Add the tomatoes and crumbled stock cube or stock powder, pour in the hot water and mix well. Stir in the tomato purée or ketchup and bring slowly to the boil. Reduce the heat to a simmer, cover the pan and leave to cook for about 1 hour, stirring occasionally.

Peel the potatoes, cut into bite-sized chunks and add to the pan, stirring gently and adding a little more hot water if needed. Cook for a further 20 minutes, then wash and slice the mushrooms, stir into the pan and cook for another 10 minutes.

Taste carefully and season with salt and pepper if needed. Serve topped with the crème fraîche and a sprinkle of paprika.

GRILLED OR FRIED STEAK

A special treat but it's cheaper to buy and cook at home than to eat steak in a restaurant! Different cuts of fresh and frozen steak are readily available at butchers' shops and supermarkets, and prices vary according to the cut you choose – see below.

Steaks should be at least 2.5 cm/1 inch thick, otherwise they dry up during cooking, so look carefully before you buy.

Serve with chips (cooked in the oven), grilled tomatoes and mushrooms, or new potatoes and a mixed green salad.

CUTS OF BEEF TO CHOOSE

Rump
Good flavour, quite lean. A steak is usually cut from a large slice, and should be at least 2.5 cm/1 inch thick.

Sirloin
Usually cut into individual slices, with a 'rind' of fat along the top which should be cooked and served on the steak to give it flavour. Steaks are usually at least 2.5 cm/1 inch thick, often thicker.

Fillet
Very tender, very expensive. Usually cut into small, very thick slices, at least 3–6 cm/1$^1/_2$–2$^1/_2$ inches.

Takes 2–3 minutes to prepare
For cooking time – see opposite

Allow 175–225 g/6–8 oz steak per serving, according to appetite
A little cooking oil or butter

GRILLED

Heat the grill. Put the steak on the greased grid of the grill pan and brush or wipe it with the oil or butter. Cook on one side, then turn it over carefully (do not stab the meat), brush or wipe the other side with the oil or butter, and cook to suit your taste:

Minute steak: 1 minute cooking on each side – very rare or blue.

'Rare' steak: 2–4 minutes each side, depending on thickness.

Medium steak: Cook as 'rare', then lower the heat for a further 3–4 minutes each side.

Well done steak: Cook as 'rare', then lower the heat for a further 4–5 minutes each side.

FRIED

Heat the frying pan gently. Put a little oil or fat in the pan. Add the steak, and cook over a medium-high heat, as for grilled steak above. Serve immediately with chosen vegetables.

Sausages and beefburgers can be cooked with the steak. Thick sausages may need a bit longer to cook than the steak, so put them under the grill or in the frying pan first, then add the steak. (See page 139.) Cut tomatoes in half and grill under the steak in the grill pan, or fry in the frying pan with the meat for 3–5 minutes. Mushrooms are best cooked in the bottom of the grill pan with a little butter, with the meat juices dripping onto them, or they can be fried in the frying pan with the steak. They will take 3–5 minutes, according to size.

10
A LITTLE LAMB

Best quality lamb is delicious but can be quite expensive. Leg and shoulder are the dearest joints of lamb, with leg costing more than shoulder. These are 'special occasion' meals, and recipes can be found in the 'Sunday Lunch' section.

Lamb chops (loin, chump and leg chops are the big ones) make a quickly cooked tasty meal, but are relatively expensive, while cutlets are small chops and are popular grilled at a barbecue as they cook quickly and can easily be hand held to eat.

Stewing lamb is much cheaper and can be bought already cut into pieces, ready to make into a stew or hotpot, or can be bought as small cutlets for stewing and cooked on the bone. Lamb stews need long, slow cooking, but make really delicious and filling meals with plenty of flavour.

LAMB CHOPS – GRILLED OR FRIED

Serves 1

Choose lean chops, but remember that lamb is basically a fatty kind of meat, and the fat gives the meat a good flavour. Chump and loin chops are larger than cutlets. Very small cutlets are sold in some supermarkets as 'breakfast chops', so decide how hungry you are feeling when you choose your chop.

Sausages or beefburgers can be cooked with the chops. Grill or fry the sausages first as they take longer to cook than the lamb. Tomatoes, mushrooms, new potatoes and peas go well with it too. Traditionally mint sauce (see page 231), mint jelly, redcurrant jelly or onion sauce (see page 229) are served with lamb.

Takes 12–17 minutes

1 chump or loin chop or 1–2 lamb cutlets
Little oil

GRILLED

Heat the grill. Brush or rub both sides of the chop with a smear of the oil. Place the chop on the greased grid of the grill pan and grill for 8–10 minutes, according to its size and your taste, turning the meat so that it browns evenly on both sides. Lamb is traditionally served pink and underdone in the middle, and brown and crispy on the outside, but cook the chops how you like them.

FRIED

Heat a little oil in a frying pan over a medium heat. Put the chops in the pan and fry, turning several times, for 8–10 minutes, until the chops are brown and crispy and cooked according to taste.

SHEPHERD'S PIE

Serves 1

A very popular and cheap-to-make dish. Follow the Cottage Pie recipe (see page 182), but use lamb mince instead of beef.

IRISH STEW WITH DUMPLINGS

Serves 2

This should satisfy even the hungriest Irishman, especially when eaten on St Patrick's Day. It makes a substantial meal on its own, and the peas and sweetcorn, though not strictly traditional, add a bit of colour to the finished dish. Serve with potatoes (if you're really hungry) and a green vegetable.

Takes about 2 $^1/_2$ hours

350 g/12 oz stewing lamb, bought cut into 2.5 cm/1 inch
   cubes
1 tbsp oil (for frying)
1 tbsp flour (for thickening)
2 onions – peeled and sliced
2 carrots – peeled and sliced
1–2 potatoes – peeled and cut into bite-sized chunks
1 lamb (or vegetable) stock cube or 2 tsp stock powder
275–425 ml/$^1/_2$–$^3/_4$ pint/2–3 cups boiling water
$^1/_2$ tsp dried mixed herbs
3–4 tbsp frozen peas
3–4 tbsp canned sweetcorn (drained)

For the dumplings
100 g/4 oz/4 heaped tbsp SELF-RAISING flour
Salt and pepper
50 g/2 oz/2 tbsp shredded suet

Trim any excess fat off the pieces of lamb. Heat the oil in a large, heavy saucepan or flameproof casserole over a moderate heat. Add the lamb pieces, stir in the thickening flour and fry together for 3–4 minutes, stirring to brown on all sides.

Add the onions and fry for a further 3–4 minutes to soften. Mix in the carrots and potatoes. Dissolve the stock cube or stock powder in a little of the hot water and gradually stir it into the stew, adding enough hot water to just cover the meat and vegetables. Stir in the dried herbs and stir gently until the stew is just simmering.

Reduce the heat, cover the pan and simmer over a low heat for $1^{1}/_{2}$ hours, stirring occasionally and adding extra water if it gets too dry.

Make the dumplings
Mix the self-raising flour, salt, pepper and suet together in a bowl. Gradually add just enough cold water to make a dough – like soft putty or plasticine. Divide the dough into four pieces, and shape into round dumplings

Stir the peas and sweetcorn into the stew. Carefully lower the dumplings onto the top, replace the lid and cook for a further 15–20 minutes, making sure the liquid is just boiling gently all the time – but do not let it boil over.

REAL LANCASHIRE HOTPOT

Serves 2

This dish may also be eaten by Yorkshiremen, and those from lesser counties!

Takes 2 hours 15 minutes

350 g/12 oz stewing lamb, bought cut into 2.5 cm/1 inch cubes
1 tbsp oil (for frying)
2 onions – peeled and sliced
1 carrot – peeled and sliced
1 small turnip (optional) – peeled and cubed
1 lamb or vegetable stock cube or 2 tsp stock powder
300 ml/$^1/_2$ pint/2 cups boiling water
2 tsp flour
Pinch of dried herbs
3 or 4 potatoes, total weight 450 g/1 lb – peeled and sliced thickly
Knob of butter

Heat the oven at 170°C/325°F/Fan 150°C/Gas Mark 3.

Cut the excess fat off the meat. Heat the oil in a large frying pan, add the lamb pieces and cook over a medium heat, stirring to brown the meat on all sides. Spoon the meat into a casserole or deep ovenproof dish.

Put the onion in the frying pan and fry for 3–4 minutes to soften. Add the carrot and turnip, and fry for a further 2–3 minutes, then add the vegetables to the meat in the casserole dish.

Dissolve the stock cube or stock powder in the hot water. Add the flour to the juices in the pan and stir, gradually adding the hot stock, stirring hard to make a smooth gravy. Add the herbs and cook until the gravy thickens, stirring all the time. Pour the gravy over the meat and vegetables to cover the meat completely.

Cover the meat and vegetables with a thick layer of potato slices, placing them so that they overlap to form a good thick crust. Dot with butter.

Cover the dish with a lid or piece of tight-fitting foil and cook in the moderate oven for about $1^1/_2$ hours.

Turn up the oven heat to 200°C/400°F/Fan 180°C/Gas Mark 6 and cook for a further 20–30 minutes to brown the potatoes.

> **QUICK TIP** *If you have to cook the hotpot on top of the stove because an oven is not available, simmer the casserole very gently on top of the stove for $1^1/_2$–2 hours, then brown the potato topping under a hot grill for a few minutes.*

BRAISED LAMB SHANK

Serves 1 (or more)

Just like you can eat in the pub, but this will be just as good and much cheaper!

Eat with jacket potatoes that can cook in the oven with the lamb and carrots or green vegetables. It is also good with mixed roast vegetables (see page 110) that can also be cooked in the oven with the lamb.

Takes 2–2 $^1/_2$ hours according to size

1 lamb shank per person – these can vary in size, so buy according to your appetite
Cooking foil
A few sprigs of fresh herbs – mint, rosemary, thyme, sage, etc
Or $^1/_2$ tsp dried herbs

Heat the oven at 180°C/350°F/Fan 160°C/Gas Mark 4. *These temperatures may vary according to your oven, so reduce the heat if the lamb seems to be cooking too fast.*

Rinse the lamb, place on a sheet of cooking foil large enough to cover the lamb, and make into a loosely wrapped parcel. Add the washed fresh herbs or sprinkle with dried herbs.

Fold the cooking foil to make a secure but loosely wrapped parcel containing the lamb, and place the parcel in a deep ovenproof casserole dish – if possible do not use a roasting tin, or the lamb may cook too quickly.

Cover the dish with a lid and roast in the moderate oven for 2–2$^1/_2$ hours, according to size. Check that the meat is not getting too brown, and reduce the oven heat if necessary.

When cooked, the lamb should be brown on the outside and *very* tender inside, so that it just falls off the bone when cut.

Carefully life the foil parcel onto a serving plate. (Take care: the foil will be hot.) Unwrap the lamb and pour the juices in the foil over the top.

If you are cooking for several people, wrap each lamb shank individually, and place the parcels together in a large casserole dish in the oven.

OVEN CHOP

Serves 1

A tasty dinner, served with a jacket potato which can cook in the oven with the casserole. This dish is equally good made with a pork chop.

Takes 35–40 minutes

1 small onion
3–4 mushrooms
$^1/_2$ tbsp oil (for frying)
1 chump or loin chop
$^1/_2$ small (230 g size) can tomatoes
Salt and pepper
Pinch of herbs

Heat the oven at 200°C/400°F/Fan 180°C/Gas Mark 6.

Peel and slice the onion. Wash and slice the mushrooms. Heat the oil in a frying pan over a medium heat. Fry the onion for 3–4 minutes to soften it. Add the chop to the pan, and cook on both sides for a few minutes to brown. Add the mushrooms and cook for another minute. Put the chop into a casserole or ovenproof dish and pour the onion and mushrooms on the top.

Heat the tomatoes in the frying pan with the meat juices. Add these to the casserole, with the salt, pepper and herbs. Cover with a lid or cooking foil. Bake in the hot oven for 30 minutes, removing the lid for the last 15 minutes to reduce the sauce to make it thicker.

If serving with a jacket potato, scrub and prick the potato, and cook it in boiling water for 15 minutes. Drain the potato. Lift it out carefully and put it into the oven to bake with the casserole.

11

PORK

Pork is a really good buy, as it is usually much cheaper than beef and the better cuts of lamb. It is a nice rich meat, so it makes a good filling winter meal without costing too much.

It is important that pork is cooked thoroughly (it is better overcooked than underdone), and must never, ever, be served pink, as rare pork can make you very ill. The meat must look pale-coloured right through. Leftover roast pork should not be reheated, but stored in the fridge and eaten cold the next day. If you are heating cooked pork dishes in a sauce, make sure the pork is really re-cooked right through to kill any bacteria, not just warmed up.

Leg, shoulder and loin of pork are the more expensive cuts. They are usually cut into roasting joints and are far too much for one person but they're great for a lunch or dinner party. Details of how to cook them are given under 'Sunday Lunch' Dishes.

Grilled pork chops and pork steaks can be served with roast potatoes and vegetables to make a 'Sunday Lunch' for one, with all the trimmings, or made into delicious dishes cooked in lovely sauces. Stewing pork can be used to make very economical winter casseroles or stews.

PORK CHOP – GRILLED OR FRIED

Serves 1

Quick and easy, and not too expensive. Tastes good with sauté potatoes, a grilled or fried tomato, pineapple rings or a spoonful of apple
sauce. Pork is better grilled, as it can be a bit greasy, but frying is quite
acceptable if you don't have a grill. Whichever way you choose to
cook it, make sure it is cooked thoroughly: the juices must run clear,
not pink, and the meat must be pale-coloured right through.
Undercooked pork can make you ill, so do cook it thoroughly.

Takes 14–16 minutes

1 pork chop
Little oil or butter
$^1/_2$ tsp dried mixed herbs or dried sage
1 tomato or 1–2 pineapple rings or 1 tbsp apple sauce
Cooked, cold boiled potatoes to sauté

Heat the grill or heat a frying pan over a moderate heat with a
smear of oil. Rub both sides of the chop with the oil or butter, and
sprinkle with the herbs. Either put the chop under the hot grill,
turning frequently, until brown and crispy, for 12–15 minutes (low-
ering the heat if the chop starts getting too brown); or put the chop
into the hot frying pan and fry over a moderate heat for 12–15
minutes, turning frequently, until brown and cooked thoroughly.

ACCOMPANIMENTS

Cut the tomato in half, dot with butter and put under the grill or
into the frying pan for the last 3–4 minutes of cooking time. Or
put the pineapple slices on top of the chop under the grill or in
the frying pan for 1–2 minutes to warm slightly. Or prepare the
apple sauce in advance from the recipe on page 230 (or use apple
sauce from a jar or can from the supermarket). Fry the sauté potatoes while the chop is cooking (see page 97). If you have only one
frying pan, you can cook them in the pan with the chop.

MUSTARD-GLAZED PORK CHOP

Serves 1

A tangy hot grilled chop. Serve with new or sauté potatoes and a green vegetable.

Takes 15–20 minutes

1 tsp mustard
1 tsp brown sugar
Knob of butter
1 pork chop

Heat the grill.

Mix the mustard, sugar and small knob of butter together in a cup. Spread this mixture over both sides of the chop.

Cook the chop under the hot grill, turning frequently, until brown and crispy (12–15 minutes). Lower the heat if the chop gets too brown too quickly. The pork must be cooked right through. The juices must run clear not pink, and the meat must be pale-coloured right through and the chop should look brown and crisp on the outside.

PORK IN CIDER

Serves 1

Rich and delicious. The smell of the meal cooking gives you a real appetite – why not make enough for two people? This is good eaten with a jacket potato that can cook in the oven with the pork – see page 98.

Takes about 1 hour

2–3 tsp cooking oil
1 pork steak or pork chop (preferably a loin chop)
1 small onion – peeled and finely chopped
1 small apple – peeled, cored and chopped
$^1/_2$–1 cup cider
Pinch of dried mixed herbs, sage or thyme
1 tbsp crème fraîche, plain yogurt or double cream

Heat the oven at 180°C/350°F/Fan 160°C/Gas Mark 4.

Heat 1 tsp oil in a frying pan over a moderate heat, and fry the pork for 4–5 minutes, turning to brown both sides. Place in a casserole or deep ovenproof dish.

Add a little more oil to the pan and fry the onion and apple together for 4–5 minutes, stirring until soft. Add to the meat in the casserole.

Pour $^1/_2$ cup of cider into the frying pan, heat gently, stirring in all the meat and vegetable juices, and pour the sauce into the casserole. Add enough extra cider to just cover the meat. Season with dried herbs.

Cover the dish with a lid or cooking foil and bake in the moderate oven for 35–45 minutes, until the pork is tender and the sauce has thickened.

Stir in the crème fraîche, yogurt or double cream and serve.

QUICK TIP *If you don't have an oven, this can be cooked very, very gently in a covered saucepan on top of the stove for 45 minutes. Check occasionally so that the sauce doesn't boil dry (add a little more liquid if necessary).*

SWEET AND SOUR PORK

Serves 1

Quick to cook and delicious to eat. Serve with boiled or fried rice.

Takes 30 minutes

175–225 g/6–8 oz pork steak or pork fillet
   (more expensive)
2–3 tsp cooking oil
1 clove of garlic – squashed – or $^1/_4$ tsp garlic powder/paste
1 or 2 salad onions – trimmed, washed and sliced
$^1/_4$ green, red or yellow pepper – washed and sliced
2 or 3 mushrooms – washed and halved
2–3 tinned pineapple rings – cut into quarters
1 large tomato – washed and sliced
3 or 4 mangetout or sugar snap pea pods – left whole

Sweet and sour sauce
2 tsp flour
1 tbsp sugar
1 tsp soy sauce
2 tbsp vinegar
$^1/_2$ pork stock cube or 1 tsp stock powder dissolved in
   $^1/_2$ cup of boiling water

Prepare the boiled or fried rice – see page 116.

Cut the pork into 3 cm/1 inch cubes. Heat the oil in a frying pan over a moderate heat, add the pork and garlic and fry for 4–5 minutes, stirring to brown the meat on all sides. Reduce the heat and continue to cook the meat for a further 10 minutes, gradually stirring in the onions, pepper, mushrooms, pineapple, tomato and pea pods, stirring and turning them gently, until all the vegetables are cooked and softened but not soggy and overcooked.

Spoon the pork and vegetables into a serving dish and keep warm.

Quickly make the sweet and sour sauce
Mix the flour and sugar to a runny paste with the soy sauce and vinegar. Dissolve the stock cube or powder in the boiling water and stir into the sauce. Pour the sauce into the frying pan and cook gently, stirring all the time until the sauce thickens. Pour the sauce over the meat and vegetables and serve.

WINTER PORK CASSEROLE

Serves 2

A really hearty winter dish, simmered on top of the stove so you don't need an oven. Use the cheaper stewing pork or boned pork shoulder. This recipe makes enough for two meals as the gravy may dry up during cooking if you only make a small amount. Serve nice and hot with potatoes, pasta, rice or noodles.

Takes 1 $^1/_2$ hours

3 tsp cooking oil
275–350 g/10–12 oz stewing pork – cut into 3 cm/1 inch cubes
1 small onion – peeled and sliced
1 leek – washed and sliced, saving as much green top as possible
About 150 ml/$^1/_4$ pint/1 cup beer or lager
2 carrots – peeled and sliced into 1 cm/$^1/_2$ inch rings
50 g/2 oz mushrooms – slice if large, leave small ones whole
1 or 2 tomatoes – washed and cut into quarters
$^1/_2$ tsp mixed dried herbs
2 tsp flour
Salt and pepper
Chopped parsley

Heat the oil in a flameproof casserole dish or heavy saucepan. Add the pork pieces and fry over a moderate heat for 3–4 minutes, stirring to brown the meat on all sides.

Add the onion and leek and fry for another 2–3 minutes to soften the vegetables, but do not let them brown.

Stir in most of the beer or lager and let it bubble for a few seconds, then stir in the carrots, mushrooms and tomatoes and season with the mixed herbs.

Mix the flour to a smooth, runny paste with a little beer or lager, and stir this into the casserole, stirring gently until the gravy thickens.

Cover the pan with a lid and simmer over a *very* gentle heat for about an hour, checking occasionally to make sure that the casserole is not too dry – add a little more beer, lager or water if needed.

Check that the pork is cooked and tender – taste carefully (it will be very hot) and adjust the seasoning to taste. Serve nice and hot.

FOIL WRAPPED PORK PACKET

Serves 1

An easy meal, without much washing up! Serve with potatoes and carrots or a green vegetable.

Takes 1 hour

1–2 tbsp uncooked raw rice or 3 tbsp cold cooked rice
2 tbsp frozen peas
$^1/_2$ small onion – peeled and finely chopped
1 tomato – cut into quarters
2 tbsp sweetcorn
2 mushrooms – washed and sliced
1 tsp Hoisin, soy or Worcester sauce
Cooking foil
1 pork chop or pork steak
Butter for greasing
1–2 tsp white wine or water

Heat the oven at 180°C/350°F/Fan 160°C/Gas Mark 4.

Cook the raw rice – see page 116 – and drain.

Put the frozen peas into a basin, cover with boiling water to defrost and drain at once. Add the rice, onion, tomato quarters, sweetcorn and mushrooms and mix gently with the chosen sauce.

Cut a large square of cooking foil, large enough to wrap the meat and mixture loosely. Grease the foil with the butter, and place the chop or pork steak in the middle. Pile the rice mixture on top of the meat and add the wine or water.

Fold into a packet or envelope, sealing the joins so that it doesn't leak and put onto a baking tin. Bake in the moderate oven for 35–40 minutes. Open carefully as there will be steam inside.

12

'SUNDAY LUNCH' DISHES

This section shows simply and clearly how to cook the traditional Sunday lunch: how to roast beef, chicken, lamb and pork. For those who don't eat meat, I've included a recipe for a Nut Roast. At the end, there are also recipes on how to make gravy and all the different sauces that accompany the various meats. All the traditional 'Sunday Lunch' recipes are for several people – according to the size of joint you buy – which is useful when you have weekend visitors.

ROAST BEEF

Very English, it should be served to celebrate St George's Day! It's best if several people can share a roast beef joint, as a very small joint is not a good buy, for it tends to shrink and dry up during cooking. Therefore you get much better value with a larger joint which should turn out to be moist and delicious.

Joints to choose for Roasting

Topside
Lean

Sirloin
Delicious, but it does have a fair amount of fat around the lean meat.

Rolled Rib
May be a little cheaper than sirloin.

Choose a joint of beef that looks appetising with clear, bright red lean meat and firm pale-cream fat. A good joint must have a little fat with it, or it will be too dry when roasted.

Make sure you know the weight of the joint you buy, as cooking time depends on the weight. *You should allow approximately 175 g/ 6 oz uncooked weight of beef per person*, so a joint weighing 1–1.5 kg/ $2^1/_2$–3 lb should provide 6–8 helpings (remember you can save some cold meat for dinner the next day).

For underdone 'rare' beef, allow 15 minutes per 450g/1 lb plus an extra 15 minutes.

For medium-done beef, allow 20 minutes per 450 g/1 lb plus an extra 20 minutes.

Remember that a small joint will cook through quicker, as it is not so thick as a big joint, so allow slightly less time.

Serve beef with Yorkshire pudding (see page 227), horseradish sauce, gravy, roast potatoes and assorted vegetables or a green salad.

Heat the oven at 200°C/400°F/Fan 180°C/Gas Mark 6.

Place the joint in a greased roasting tin, with a little lard, dripping, margarine or oil on top. The joint, or the whole tin, may be covered with foil to help keep the meat moist. Roast in the hot oven for the appropriate time as explained opposite. Test that the meat is cooked by stabbing it with a fork or vegetable knife, and note the colour of the juices that run out: the redder the juice, the more rare the meat. When the meat is cooked, lift it out carefully onto a hot serving plate and make the gravy (see page 226).

For the roast potatoes: calculate when the joint will be ready and allow the potatoes 45–60 minutes roasting time, according to size. They can be roasted around the joint or in a separate tin in the oven. (See page 96.)

ROAST CHICKEN

It may sound odd, but larger chickens are far more economical; you get more meat and less bone for your money, so it's worth sharing a chicken between several people, and keeping some cold for the next day (put it in the fridge and don't keep it too long). The scrappy bits left on the carcass can be chopped up and used to make a risotto.

Before cooking a frozen chicken, make sure the chicken is completely defrosted by leaving it out at room temperature for several hours according to the instructions on the wrapper. It can be soaked in cold (not hot) water to get rid of the last bits of ice and hurry the thawing process but do not try to thaw it in hot water as the chicken will be tough when cooked. (See page 167.)

A 900–1100 g/2–2 1/2 lb chicken will serve 2–3 people, while a 1.3–1.8 kg/3–4 lb chicken will serve 4–6 people, according to appetite.

Make sure you know the weight of the bird as cooking time depends on the weight.

Allow 20 minutes per 450 g/1 lb plus 20 minutes extra. Very small chickens (900–1100 g/2–2 1/2 lb) may only need 15 minutes per 450 g/1 lb plus 15 minutes extra.

Chicken is traditionally served with chipolata sausages, thyme and parsley stuffing and bread sauce. We like apple sauce or cranberry sauce with it as well. Roast potatoes, parsnips, carrots and sprouts are tasty with chicken in the winter, while new potatoes and peas make a good summer dinner.

1 chicken (completely defrosted)
Small potato (optional)
Oil and butter (for roasting)
Cooking foil

Heat the oven at 200°C/400°F/Fan 180°C/Gas Mark 6. Rinse the chicken in cold water and dry with kitchen paper. It is now thought best to roast chicken without putting stuffing inside. The stuffing sometimes causes the meat not to be thoroughly cooked. If you are making stuffing, cook it separately in a greased dish, according to the instructions on the packet (see page 232), or only put a little inside the chicken. I sometimes put a small, peeled raw potato inside the chicken as the steam from the potato keeps the chicken moist.

Spread the butter and oil liberally over the chicken (you can cover the breast and legs with butter papers if you have any) and either wrap the chicken loosely in foil and put it into a roasting tin, or put it into a greased roasting tin and cover the tin with foil. Put the chicken in the tin into the hot oven. Calculate the cooking time so that the rest of the dinner is ready at the same time.

Sausages, roast potatoes and parsnips can be cooked round the chicken or in a separate roasting tin. Sausages will take 20–30 minutes; potatoes and parsnips about 45 minutes to 1 hour.

Remove or open the foil for the last 15 minutes of cooking time to brown the chicken. Test that the chicken is cooked by prodding it with a pointed knife or fork in the thickest part, inside the thigh. The juices should run clear; if they are still pink, cook for a little longer. Remove the chicken carefully onto a hot serving plate, and use the juices in the tin to make the gravy. (See page 226.)

ROAST LAMB

Leg and shoulder are both expensive joints. Shoulder is cheaper than leg but tends to be more fatty. These joints are sold on the bone or boned and rolled, so allow more weight of meat for each person if you buy lamb on the bone than if you buy it rolled – though carving a shoulder of lamb can provide a good cabaret.

Allow 225 g/8 oz lamb on the bone per person so a 1 kg/2 1/2 lb joint will serve 4 people.
Allow 175 g/6 oz boned rolled lamb per person so a 1 kg/2 1/2 lb joint will serve 6 people.

The traditional accompaniments for lamb are mint sauce, mint jelly, redcurrant jelly or onion sauce. Serve with roast potatoes, parsnips or other vegetables.

ROAST LEG OR SHOULDER OF LAMB

You don't have to buy a whole leg or shoulder; half legs and shoulders, or a piece of a very large joint can be bought. Make sure you know the weight of the meat you buy as cooking time depends on the weight.

Allow 20 minutes per 450 g/1 lb plus an extra 20 minutes

Joint of leg or shoulder of lamb
Oil or dripping (for roasting)
2–3 cloves of garlic (optional)
2–3 sprigs of rosemary (optional)

Heat the oven at 200°C/400°F/Fan 180°C/Gas Mark 6.

Place the joint in a roasting tin, with a little oil or dripping. If you like the flavour of garlic, you can insert one or two peeled cloves under the skin of the meat, near the bone, to impart a garlic flavour to the meat, but lamb has a lovely flavour so this is not really necessary. Rosemary sprigs can be used in the same way.

Cover the joint, or the whole tin, with cooking foil. (This helps to stop the meat shrivelling up.) Roast it in the hot oven for the calculated time, removing the foil for the last 20–30 minutes of the cooking time to brown the meat if it is a bit pale under the foil. Roast potatoes and parsnips can be cooked with the joint for the last hour of cooking time.

Test that the lamb is cooked at the end of the cooking time by stabbing it with a fork or a vegetable knife. Lamb is traditionally served pink in the middle, but many people prefer it cooked more; it is entirely a matter of personal preference. The meat juices should run slightly tinged with pink for underdone lamb, and run clear when the lamb is better cooked. When the meat is cooked satisfactorily, lift it carefully onto a hot serving plate and make the gravy. Serve with mint sauce.

ROAST PORK

Most pork joints are now sold boned and rolled so are nice and easy to carve.

JOINTS TO CHOOSE FOR ROASTING

Leg: the leanest and most expensive.

Shoulder: cheaper and just as tasty.

Loin: chops, left in one piece, not cut up.

Allow about 250 g/8 oz per serving: a 1.12–1.35 kg/2 $^1/_2$–3 lb joint should serve 4–6 people. Make sure you know the weight of your joint, as the cooking time depends on the weight.

Allow 25 minutes per 450 g/1 lb plus 25 minutes extra.

Pork is traditionally served with sage and onion stuffing, and apple sauce. Also serve it with roast potatoes and parsnips or other vegetables.

Heat the oven at 200°C/400°F/Fan 180°C/Gas Mark 6 so that the joint goes into a hot oven, to make the crackling crisp. Rub the pork skin with oil, and sprinkle with salt to give the crackling a good flavour. Place the joint in the roasting tin with a little oil or fat to stop it sticking to the tin. Put the tin into the hot oven and calculate the cooking time so that the rest of the dinner can be ready at the right time.

After 20 minutes or so, when the crackling is looking crisp, the joint or the whole tin can be covered with foil to stop the meat getting too brown (smaller joints will brown more easily). Roast potatoes or parsnips can be cooked around the meat for the last hour of the cooking time, or in a separate roasting tin. Cook the stuffing in a greased dish, according to the instructions on the packet (see page 232).

Test that the meat is cooked at the end of the cooking time: the juices should run clear when prodded with a knife or fork. If they are still pink, cook for a bit longer. Pork must be cooked right through (it is better overcooked than underdone) as rare pork can cause food poisoning. The meat should be pale-coloured, not pink. When it is completely cooked, lift it onto a hot serving plate and make the gravy.

NUT ROAST

Serves 2

The traditional vegetarian 'Sunday Lunch' meal that everyone has heard of. This recipe makes enough for two portions since cold nut roast is tasty too. If you have a freezer, the second portion can be frozen, uncooked, for use later. Serve with tomato sauce.

You can also buy 'fresh chilled' nut roast ready to bake at most large supermarkets.

Takes 45 minutes (individual dishes)
60 minutes (larger dishes)

1 onion
1 stick of celery
100 g/4 oz/1 very full cup mixed nuts – roughly chopped (a processor or liquidiser is useful for this)
2 large fresh tomatoes or use the tomatoes from a small (230 g) can of tomatoes (you can use the juice as an aperitif)
1 tbsp oil and a knob of butter (for frying)
75 g/3 oz/3 full cups fresh wholemeal breadcrumbs
Salt and pepper
$^1/_2$ tsp mixed herbs
Pinch of chilli powder
1 egg
Piece of foil (for covering the dishes)

Heat the oven at 200°C/400°F/Fan 180°C/Gas Mark 6. Grease two individual dishes or one larger tin. (Foil dishes are useful for this.)

Peel and chop the onion. Wash and chop the celery. Chop the nuts. Chop the tomatoes.

Heat the oil and butter in a large frying pan or saucepan over a moderate heat and fry the onion and celery gently for 4–5 minutes until softened but not browned. Remove from the heat. Add the nuts, breadcrumbs, chopped tomatoes, salt, pepper, herbs and chilli powder.

Beat the egg in a small basin or cup and stir into the mixture. Taste and adjust the seasoning and herbs if necessary.

Spoon into the well-greased tins and cover lightly with greased cooking foil.

Bake in the hot oven as follows:
Small tins for 20–30 minutes, removing the foil after 15 minutes;
Large tins for 45–60 minutes, removing the foil after 30 minutes.

GRAVY

Often the meat juices alone from grilled or fried meat make a tasty sauce poured over the meat. But if you want to make a 'real' gravy, remember that the more flour you use, the thicker the gravy will be. The liquid can be any mixture of water, vegetable water, wine, sherry, beer or cider.

Takes 4 minutes

1–2 tsp flour and 1 tsp gravy flavouring powder or 2 tsp gravy granules
150 ml/$^1/_4$ pint/1 cup water or vegetable water and/or wine, beer, sherry or cider
Any juices from the meat

Mix the flour and the gravy flavouring powder (if used) into a smooth paste with a little of the cold water, wine, cider, sherry or even beer (depending on what you're drinking). Add the rest of the water and the meat juices from the roasting tin.

Pour the mixture into a small saucepan and bring to the boil, stirring all the time. Stir gravy granules, if used, straight into the hot liquid. Add more liquid if the gravy is too thick or more flour mixture if it is too thin.

To thicken the gravy used in stews and casseroles, make the gravy as above. Stir the mixture into the stew or casserole and bring to the boil so that the gravy can thicken as it cooks.

YORKSHIRE PUDDING

Individual Yorkshire puddings are baked in patty (bun) tins, but a larger pudding can be cooked in any baking tin (not one with a loose base!), but they do not cook very well in a pyrex-type dish.

Takes 25 minutes (small); 40–45 minutes (large)

4 heaped tbsp PLAIN flour
Pinch of salt
1 egg
300 ml/$^1/_2$ pint/2 cups milk
Little oil or fat

Put the flour and salt in a basin. Use a clean saucepan if you do not have a large basin. Add the egg and beat into the flour, gradually adding the milk, and beating to make a smooth batter. (The easiest way of doing this is with a hand or electric mixer, but with a bit more effort you get just as good a result using a whisk, a wooden spoon or even a fork.) Beat well.

Heat the oven at 200°C/400°F/Fan 180°C/Gas Mark 6.

Put the tins, with the fat in, on the top shelf of the oven for a few minutes to get hot. Give the batter a final whisk and pour it into the tins. Bake until firm and golden brown. Try not to open the oven door for the first 10 minutes so that the puds rise well. If you want meat and puds ready together, start cooking the puds 25 minutes before the meat is ready for small puds, 40–45 minutes before for large puds.

WHITE SAUCE

This is a quick way to make a basic sauce to which you can add other ingredients or flavourings.

Takes 5 minutes

2 tsp flour
150 ml/$^1/_4$ pint/1 cup milk
12 g/$^1/_2$ oz butter or margarine
Salt and pepper

Put the flour in a large mug or small basin. Mix it into a runny paste with 1 tbsp of the milk. Boil the rest of the milk in a saucepan. Pour it onto the well-stirred flour mixture, stirring all the time. Pour the mixture back into the saucepan, return to the heat and bring to the boil, stirring all the time until the sauce thickens. Beat in the butter or margarine. Season with salt and pepper.

CHEESE SAUCE
Grate 25–50 g/1–2 oz cheese. Add to the white sauce with the butter and add a dash of mustard if you have any.

PARSLEY SAUCE
Wash and drain a handful of sprigs of parsley. Chop them finely with a knife or scissors and add to the sauce with the salt and pepper.

ONION SAUCE

A quick and easy method. Onion sauce is traditionally served with lamb, and is also tasty poured over cauliflower.

Takes 25 minutes

1 onion
150 ml/$^1/_4$ pint/1 cup water
2 tsp flour
150 ml/$^1/_4$ pint/1 cup milk
Knob of butter
Salt and pepper

Peel and finely chop the onion. Put it into a small saucepan, with the cup of water. Bring to the boil, then lower the heat and cook gently for 10–15 minutes until the onion is soft.

In a bowl mix the flour into a paste with a little of the milk. Gradually add this into the onion mixture, stirring all the time as the mixture thickens. Add more milk, until the sauce is just thick enough – not runny, but not like blancmange. Beat in the knob of butter, and season with the salt and pepper. Serve hot.

'INSTANT' SAUCE MIX

Several makes of sauce mix are widely available at supermarkets. Follow the instructions on the packet, and only make up as much sauce as is needed for the recipe. Keep the rest of the packet for later, tightly closed, in a dry cupboard or fridge.

BREAD SAUCE

Serve it with chicken. I generally use a packet of bread sauce mix, which is very easy to make, cooks quickly and tastes good, especially with the addition of a little extra butter and a spoonful of cream. Allow 150 ml/$\frac{1}{4}$ pint/1 cup of milk for 1–2 servings; 300 ml/$\frac{1}{2}$ pint/2 cups of milk will make enough sauce for 2–4 people, according to your appetites.

1 packet bread sauce mix (you only need to use part of the packet, but the rest will keep in the store cupboard)
150 ml/$\frac{1}{4}$ pint/1 cup milk
Knob of butter (optional)
2 tsp cream (optional

Make the sauce according to the instructions on the packet. Stir in the butter and cream just before serving. Leftover sauce will keep overnight in the fridge and can be used on cold chicken sandwiches.

APPLE SAUCE

You can buy jars or tins or apple purée, but it is cheaper and very easy to make your own. Apple sauce is served with roast pork or poultry.

Takes 10–15 minutes

1–2 cooking apples
2–3 tbsp water
1–2 tbsp sugar

Peel, core and slice the apples. Put them in a saucepan with the water and bring to the boil gently. Simmer for 5–10 minutes until the apples are soft (do not let them boil dry). Add the sugar to taste (be careful, the apples will be *very* hot) and mash with a fork until smooth.

MINT SAUCE

You can buy jars of mint sauce at the supermarket but I think they taste better if you re-mix the sauce with a little sugar and 1–2 tsp of fresh vinegar. Mint sauce is traditionally served with lamb.

'BOUGHT' MINT SAUCE

3–4 'bought' mint sauce
1 tsp granulated sugar
1–2 tsp vinegar

Mix all the above ingredients together in a small glass or dish.

'FRESH' MINT SAUCE

Handful of fresh mint sprigs
2–3 tbsp vinegar (wine vinegar if you have it)
1–2 tsp granulated sugar

Strip the leaves from the stems. Wash well, drain and chop the mint as finely as possible. Mix the mint, vinegar and sugar in a small glass or dish, and serve with the lamb. This sauce will keep in a small, covered jar in the fridge.

STUFFING

Traditionally sage and onion stuffing goes with pork, while thyme and parsley goes with chicken, but any mixture of herbs is tasty.

Takes 35–45 minutes

1 packet (75 g/3 oz size) stuffing
A little butter or margarine
Hot water – you can use water from the kettle or
    vegetable water

Heat the oven at 200°C/400°F/Fan 180°C/Gas Mark 6.

Make up the stuffing according to the packet. Grease an oven-proof dish, put the stuffing in the dish, dot with the butter or margarine. Bake in the hot oven with the joint for 30–40 minutes until crispy on top.

13

PUDDINGS AND CAKES

A few cheap and easy recipes for those with a sweet tooth.

There are lots of delicious fresh, chilled and frozen desserts, gooey gateaux, mouthwatering cakes and sticky buns available in the shops to provide an instant treat, but they can be rather expensive and it's easy to make a quick pudding for yourself when you fancy something sweet, and top it with a dollop of homemade sauce as well!

For a really quick and easy 'homemade' cake, scan the packets of cake, pudding and biscuit mixes on the supermarket shelves. With the addition of water, and sometimes a little butter and an egg, you can easily produce superb cakes – my favourites are lovely gooey Chocolate Brownies and Chocolate Chip Cookies, eaten fresh and warm from the oven.

QUICK CHOCOLATE SAUCE – FOR ICE-CREAM

Serves 1

Fast, easy and most effective. It has a lovely, chocolatey flavour but is not too rich.

Takes 5 minutes

1 chocolate bar (25–50 g/1–2 oz size)
1 tsp cold water

Break the chocolate into a pottery or pyrex basin or jug and add 1 tsp of water. Stand the basin in 2.5 cm/1 inch of hot water in a saucepan over a low heat and simmer gently until the chocolate melts. Stir well and pour the chocolate sauce over scoops of ice-cream.

HOT CHOCOLATE FUDGE SAUCE –
TO SERVE WITH ICE-CREAM

Serves 1

A rich fudgy sauce, delicious with vanilla, chocolate or coffee-flavoured ice-cream.

Takes 10 minutes

**50 g/2 oz chocolate chips, chocolate cake covering or a
    chocolate bar**
1 tbsp brown sugar
1 tbsp cold water
25 g/1 oz butter (unsalted is best)
2 tsp rum (optional)

Put the chocolate, sugar and water into a small saucepan, over a low heat, and stir until the chocolate melts and the mixture is smooth and creamy. Remove from the heat. Add the butter in small flakes. Beat well. Beat in the rum if used. Serve, poured over scoops of ice-cream.

If necessary, reheat the sauce later by putting it into a pyrex or a pottery basin or mug, and stand this in 2.5 cm/1 inch of hot water in a saucepan. Put the saucepan over a low heat and simmer gently until the sauce melts again, stirring well.

BANANA SPLIT

Serves 1

Full of calories, but absolutely delicious!

Takes 5 minutes (plus time for making the chocolate sauce)

1 large banana
2–3 tbsp ice-cream
1 tbsp chocolate sauce (bought or homemade – see
pages 234 or 235)
1 tbsp thick cream – spooning cream is ideal
Chopped nuts (for decoration, optional)
Chocolate sprinkles (for decoration, optional)

Split the banana in half, lengthways, then place it on a plate. Sandwich the banana halves together with spoonfuls of ice-cream. Spoon the chocolate sauce over the top. Decorate with the cream and sprinkle nuts or chocolate sprinkles on the top. Eat immediately.

FRUIT PAVLOVA

Serves 1

A super summer sweet. Make it with cream, ice-cream – or both!

Takes 5 minutes

1–2 tbsp fresh or canned fruit – raspberries, strawberries, canned peaches, mandarins, pineapple, pears
1–2 tbsp thick cream (spooning cream is good) and/or 1–2 tbsp ice-cream
1–2 meringue nests (available in packets from supermarkets)

Prepare this dish just before you are ready to eat it. Wash and drain the fresh fruit or drain the canned fruit. Spread the ice-cream over the meringue nests. Arrange the fresh or canned fruit carefully on top of the cream or ice-cream. Decorate with a spoonful of thick cream. Serve at once.

PANCAKES

These can be sweet or savoury, and are delicious any day, not just on Shrove Tuesday (Pancake Day). Sweet pancakes are traditionally served sprinkled with 1 tsp sugar and a squeeze of lemon. For sweet and savoury fillings, see page 35.

Takes 10 minutes (plus 1 minute per pancake cooking time)

100 g/4 oz/4 heaped tbsp plain flour
1 egg
300 ml/$1/_2$ pint/2 cups milk
Oil for frying – not butter

Prepare the filling if used. Put the flour into a bowl. Add the egg and beat it into the flour. Gradually add the milk and beat to make a smooth batter. (The easiest way to do this is with a hand or electric mixer, but with a bit of effort you get just as good a result using a wooden spoon or even a fork.)

Heat a clean frying pan over a moderate heat, and when hot, but not burning, grease the pan with a smear of oil, approximately $1/_2$ tsp. Pour in a little batter, enough to cover the pan thinly. Tilt the pan to spread the batter over it. Fry briskly, until just set on top, and lightly browned underneath, shaking the pan occasionally to stop the pancake sticking – this will only take a few moments.

Toss the pancake or flip it over with a knife, and fry for a few more moments to cook the other side. Turn it out onto a warm plate. Sprinkle with lemon and sugar, or add the filling, and roll up or fold into four.

Pancakes taste best eaten at once, straight from the pan, but they can be filled, rolled up and kept warm while you cook the rest. Wipe the pan with a pad of kitchen paper, reheat and regrease the pan, and cook the next pancake as before.

SYRUPY PEACHES

Serves 1

Make this lovely pudding when fresh peaches are cheap in the shops. Serve hot with cream or ice-cream. (This dish can be prepared, but not cooked, in advance, the cold fruit being left to soak in the syrup, and then put in the oven to cook while you are eating your first course.)

Takes 15 minutes

2 tbsp brown sugar
$^1/_2$ cup water
1–2 peaches

Heat the oven at 180°C/350°F/Fan 160°C/Gas Mark 4. Make the syrup: put the brown sugar and water into a small saucepan, bring to the boil, stirring occasionally, and simmer gently for 3–4 minutes to dissolve the sugar. Wash the peaches (do not peel) and cut them in half, from top to bottom. Remove the stones. Put the peaches into an ovenproof dish with the cut sides face upwards, and pour the hot syrup over the fruit, spooning it into the holes left by the stones. Put into the warm oven for 10–15 minutes until the fruit is hot and the syrup bubbling.

GRILLED PEACHES

Serves 1

Absolutely delicious with fresh peaches, but very good with tinned fruit too. Buy cheap peaches in the summer for a treat. Serve with cream or ice-cream.

Takes 5 minutes

1–2 fresh peaches or $^1/_2$ a tin (425 g size) of peaches
25 g/1 oz butter
2 tbsp demerara sugar

Peel and slice the fresh peaches or drain and slice the tinned peaches. Butter an ovenproof dish, and place the peach slices in the dish. Sprinkle thickly with the brown sugar, dot with some butter. Place the dish under a hot grill for a minute or two so that the sugar melts and the peach slices warm through. Serve at once.

LIQUEUR ORANGES

Serves 2

Delicious, simple and rather unusual, so save it for when you are entertaining a special friend.

Takes 5 minutes to prepare + at least 1–2 hours chilling time (all day is best)

2 large sweet oranges
2 tbsp sugar
1 tbsp orange liqueur – Cointreau, Grand Marnier or
   Curaçao (you can buy a miniature bottle of liqueur)
Thick cream (optional)

Peel the oranges and scrape away any white pith. Cut the oranges into thin rings, and arrange the slices in a shallow serving dish. Sprinkle with the sugar and liqueur. Cover the dish with a plate or cling film and leave it in the fridge or in a cold place for at least an hour, but all day if possible, to chill and let the liqueur soak in. Serve on its own or with thick cream.

CHOCOLATE KRISPIES

Almost everyone likes these, and they're cheap too. Instead of the sugar and cocoa, you can use 4 tbsp drinking chocolate and only 1 tbsp sugar.

Takes 15 minutes

50 g/2 oz butter or spread
2 tbsp sugar
2 tbsp golden syrup
2 level tbsp cocoa
75 g/3 oz/3 cups cornflakes or rice krispies
12–15 paper cases

Put the butter or spread, sugar and syrup in a medium-sized saucepan, and heat over a gentle heat until melted. Stir in the cocoa (or drinking chocolate) and stir well to make a chocolate syrup. Stir in the cornflakes or krispies, and mix well to coat them thoroughly. Heap them into the paper cases and leave to set. Store in a tin or plastic box.

APPLE CRUMBLE

Serves 2–3

Use any pie fruit (plums, gooseberries, rhubarb) to make a delicious crumble, or add a small handful of raspberries, blackberries or raisins with apples, but a sugary apple crumble is very hard to beat.

Takes about 45 minutes

Topping
100 g/4 oz flour – plain or self-raising
50 g/2 oz sugar
50 g/2 oz butter or spread

Filling
250 g/$^1/_2$ lb cooking apples (or chosen pie fruit)
25–50 g/1–2 oz sugar or to taste

Heat the oven at 200°C/400°F/Fan 180°C/Gas Mark 6.

Put the flour and sugar into a bowl, add the butter or spread cut into small pieces, and rub together with your fingertips until the mixture looks like breadcrumbs.

Peel, core and thinly slice the apples, and put into a deep 0.5 litre/1 pint deep pie dish (with any extra fruit if used), adding sugar to taste. Spoon the topping over the fruit and smooth down lightly with a fork.

Stand the dish on a baking tray and cook for 20–25 minutes until the fruit is soft and the crumble is a golden brown. Serve warm with custard, cream or crème fraîche.

Wholewheat Topping

**100 g/4 oz wholewheat flour instead of plain or
self-raising flour**

50 g/2 oz brown sugar instead of granulated sugar

Scottish Oat Topping

50 g/2 oz white or wholemeal flour

50 g/2 oz porridge oats

50 g/2 oz demerara sugar

Crunchy Nut Crumble

Add 25 g/1 oz mixed nuts to any of the toppings

Other Fruit Fillings

Plums – rinse, leave whole or cut in half, but leave the stones in
the fruit – warn any guests that there will be stones in the fruit –
don't forget to count your plum stones to find out who you will
marry!

Gooseberries – rinse, top and tail. You may need extra sugar as
gooseberries can be very sour.

Rhubarb – rinse, cut off tops and rooty bits. Cut into 5 cm/2 inch
pieces. Rhubarb can also be very sour, so you may need extra
sugar.

BREAD AND BUTTER PUDDING

Serves 2–3

The school days 'afters' that everyone remembers with either delight or disgust! However, this recipe makes such a delicious warm winter pudding that I defy anyone not to enjoy it. Any leftovers can be warmed through and eaten the next day.

Takes 45 minutes + 30 minutes soaking

25–50 g/1–2 oz well-softened butter or spread
3–4 bread slices from a large loaf (white, brown or fruit)
50 g/2 oz currants, sultanas or mixed dried fruit
2 tbsp granulated sugar
1 egg
225 ml/8 fl oz milk
Few drops vanilla essence

Well butter a 0.5 litre/1 pint deep pie dish or ovenproof dish. Butter the bread slices. I like to leave the crusts on for extra crunch. Cut into triangles and arrange half the slices in an overlapping pointy layer on the base of the dish, with the butter side down.

Sprinkle with all the chosen fruit and 1 tbsp sugar. Top with the remaining bread triangles in an overlapping layer as before, but with the butter side up this time. Sprinkle the remaining sugar over the top.

Break the egg into a basin, beat well and mix in the milk and vanilla essence. Pour the egg mixture over the pudding, making sure all the bread is covered. Leave the pudding to soak for about 30 minutes until the bread has soaked up nearly all the milk – it can stand longer if needed.

Heat the oven at 170°C/325°F/Fan 150°/Gas Mark 3.

Stand the dish on a baking tray and bake in the moderate oven for 25–30 minutes until the pudding is risen and set, with a lovely crispy golden top.

Serve hot on its own or with thick cream, crème fraîche, ice cream or custard.

BOOZY POACHED PEARS

Serves 1 or 2

Choose nice large, even-sized pears and decide which syrup you prefer. The basic method of preparation for each syrup is the same. Allow 1 pear per person, but the cooked pears keep well and it's good to be able to have a second helping!

Takes 1¹/₂ hours

2 or 3 large, even-sized pears

Heat the oven at 170°C/325°F/Fan 150°/Gas Mark 3.

Wash, core and peel the pears – use a vegetable knife or apple corer to remove the core from the *base* of the pears, but leave the stalk for decoration. *It's easier to core pears before they are peeled.* Stand the pears close together in a small, deep ovenproof dish.

PEARS IN WHITE WINE

75 ml/3 fl oz white wine
75 ml/3 fl oz water
3 tbsp sugar
1 lemon

PEARS IN RED WINE

75 ml/3 fl oz red wine
75 ml/3 fl oz water
3 tbsp sugar
2 tbsp port

PEARS IN GRENADINE

75 ml/3 fl grenadine syrup (this is non-alcoholic)
2 tbsp sugar
1 lemon
$1/_4$ tsp each of cloves, cinnamon and ground nutmeg –
or to taste

Put the chosen wine or grenadine, water and sugar in a small pan over a *low* heat, adding the lemon rind and juice to the white wine or grenadine. Stir until the sugar dissolves, then allow to boil for 3–4 minutes until the syrup thickens slightly – *take care not to let it boil over.* Stir the port into the red wine and add the spices to the grenadine. Stir and pour the syrup over the pears in the dish so that it nearly covers them.

Cook in the low oven for about an hour, spooning the syrup over the pears frequently, until the pears are just softened.

Serve hot or cold, spooning some syrup over each pear and, for a real treat, top with thick cream, crème fraîche or ice-cream.

NORA'S MAGIC CHOCOLATE PUDDING

Serves 3–4

This is so delicious you'll want nice big helpings, and any leftover pudding can be kept in the fridge for tomorrow.

It's fun to make as the runny cocoa mixture poured over the top of the unbaked pudding magically turns into a fudgy chocolate sauce underneath the gooey pudding.

Takes 1–1¹/₄ hours

50 g/2 oz plain cooking chocolate
50 g/2 oz butter or spread
100 g/4 oz self-raising flour
50 g/2 oz sugar
150 ml/¹/₄ pint/1 cup milk
¹/₂ tsp vanilla essence

Sauce
100 g/4 oz soft brown sugar
3 tbsp cocoa
300 ml/¹/₂ pint/2 cups boiling water

Heat the oven at 180°C/350°F/Fan 160°C/Gas Mark 4. Well butter a 900 ml/1¹/₂ pint ovenproof dish.

Melt the chocolate and butter or spread in a bowl over a pan of simmering water, or in the microwave (check the instruction book). Put the flour and sugar into a mixing bowl, stir in the melted chocolate and butter/spread mixture, milk and vanilla essence, and beat well with a wooden spoon, to make a thick, runny batter. Pour the pudding into the prepared dish.

Make the sauce
Put the soft brown sugar and cocoa into a basin, stir in the boiling water and pour the 'sauce' gently over the pudding.

Bake in the moderate oven for 40–45 minutes until the sponge rises like magic above the chocolate fudge sauce.

Serve warm with thick cream or a dollop of vanilla or chocolate ice-cream.

INDEX

THE COMPLETE UNIVERSITY GUIDE: STUDENT FINANCE

Your guide to loans, bursaries, grants, tuition fees and preparing your own budget

by Bernard Kingston and Nicola Chalton

with a Foreword by Professor Robert Burgess, Vice-Chancellor, University of Leicester

Understand how student funding differs within England, Scotland, Wales and Northern Ireland. Get a realistic picture of all your likely outgoings – accommodation, food, travel, study costs, insurance and socialising – and work out a sensible budget.

- The latest information on all sources of student finance
- Valuable survival tips and first-hand accounts from students
- Practical advice on gap year, vacation and part-time term work

What students say about this book:
'Excellent advice and guidance.'
'Very valuable for a first time student.'
'Of great use to both students and parents.'

Make the right choices – what to study, where to study – with the help of www.thecompleteuniversityguide.co.uk

Three ways to order *Right Way* books:

(1) Visit www.constablerobinson.com and order through our website.

(2) Telephone the TBS order line on 01206 255 800.
Order lines are open Monday – Friday, 8:30am – 5:30pm.

(3) Use this order form and send a cheque made payable to **TBS Ltd** or charge
my   [ ] Visa   [ ] Mastercard   [ ] Maestro (issue no   )

Card number: _____

Expiry date: _____ Last three digits on back of card: _____

Signature: _____

(your signature is essential when paying by credit or debit card)

No. of copies	Title	Price	Total
	Complete University Guide: Student Finance	£7.99	
	Microwave Recipes for One	£4.99	
	The Curry Secret	£5.99	
	For P&P add £2.75 for the first book, 60p for each additional book **Grand Total**		 £

Name: _____
Address: _____
_____ Postcode: _____

Daytime Tel. No./Email _____
(in case of query)

**Please return forms to Cash Sales/Direct Mail Dept., The Book
Service, Colchester Road, Frating Green, Colchester CO7 7DW.**

Enquiries to readers@constablerobinson.com.

Constable and Robinson Ltd (directly or via its agents) may mail, email or
phone you about promotions or products.

[ ] Tick box if you do not want these from us [ ] or our subsidiaries.

www.constablerobinson.com